EDWARD IRVING
MAN, PREACHER, PROPHET

BY
JEAN CHRISTIE ROOT

"A man of one thought, the gospel of Christ;
A man of one purpose, the glory of God;
Content to be reckoned a madman—for Christ."
IRVING: *Missionary Sermon*

WIPF & STOCK · Eugene, Oregon

Wipf and Stock Publishers
199 W 8th Ave, Suite 3
Eugene, OR 97401

Edward Irving
Man, Preacher, Prophet
By Root, Jean Christie
ISBN 13: 978-1-60899-374-1
Publication date 1/21/2010
Previously published by Sherman, French & Co, 1912

FOREWORD

The present seems a not unfitting time to represent to candid thinkers of all creeds the man who perhaps more clearly foreshadowed the problems and truths of to-day than any other one man in his period. The author has striven by the clearest light attainable to present Edward Irving exactly as he was, and to call attention to the truths for which he so bravely and patiently "endured as seeing Him who is invisible." It has long mattered little to him personally whether men would or would not listen to the truths he saw and "with all the power within him strove to utter." [1] It mattered much to his own generation and may matter much to ours if the Church, claiming to be the conservator of Truth, continues to treat this man, "a minister of Christ, after the order of Paul," [2] as an outcast to be permanently forgotten. Rather might it not be well, if like Edward Irving, all men everywhere, inside the Church or out of it, forgetting prejudice, should honestly welcome the truth wherever they found it and follow it whithersoever it might lead them?

[1] Carlyle.
[2] Coleridge.

CONTENTS

CHAPTER | PAGE

1 *Edward Irving's Period and the Impending Changes. Heredity Preparatory Years.* . . . 1

2 *Teaching. Jean Baillie Welsh. Isabella Martin. Thomas Carlyle.* 7

3 *Prolonged Probationing. Considers Mission Work. Jean Welsh Reappears. Call to Assist Dr. Chalmers. Terrible Conditions in Glasgow. Applied Christianity Conquers.* 15

4 *Call to London. Strange Acceptance. Unparalleled Success.* . 22

5 *Decision as to Marriage. Comments by Carlyle and Mrs. Oliphant. Marriage to Miss Martin. Birth of Little Edward. Death of the Child and its Remarkable Effect on Mr. Irving. Journal Letter "To Comfort Little Edward's Mother." Perfected Union.* 28

CONTENTS

CHAPTER		PAGE
6	*Growing Influence. New Church in Regent's Square. Peculiar Dedications to Books. Unpopular Missionary Sermon.*	42
7	*Mr. Hatley Frere. Mr. Henry Drummond and Albury Conferences. Irving Declares Christ the Head of the Church and Creeds Finite.*	51
8	*Cry of Heresy. Religious Awakening in Scotland. Peculiar Manifestations. Baptism of the Holy Spirit. Advent of the "Tongues" in Scotland. First and Second Cases of Healing in Scotland (Presbyterian). Case of Miss Fancourt in London (Episcopalian). Mr. Irving's Attitude towards these Facts.*	62
9	*Other Ministers Charged with Heresy. Mr. Irving's Book, "Human Nature of Christ," Severely Handled. Advent of "Tongues" in his Church, July, 1831. Opinions of Carlyle and Others. Clear Statements by Henry Drummond and Rev. W. W. Andrews. Mr. Baxter's Defection. Modern Psycholog-*	

CONTENTS

CHAPTER		PAGE
	ical Statement Concerning "Gift of Tongues". . . .	82
10	Anxiety of Irving's Church Trustees. Irving Summoned before the London Presbytery. A Peculiar Trial. Remarkable Verdict. Deposed, May, 1832. Irving Enters Catholic Apostolic Church	101
11	Failing Health. Last Call on the Carlyles. Leaves London for Rest. Last Journey. Last Letter. "Dies unto God." Universal Mourning. . . .	113
12	Appreciations by S. T. Coleridge, Thomas Carlyle, Frederick D. Maurice, Extract from a Personal Letter, Rev. James Hamilton, D. D., Rev. W. W. Andrews, Rev. Geo. Leon Walker, D. D., Barry Cornwall, Christian Remembrancer, Fraser's Magazine, January, 1835, North British Review, Vol. XXXIX (Attributed to Dr. Hanna), London Quarterly Review, Vol. XIX, Macmillan's Magazine, Vol. VI (Attributed to Rev. Robert Story). . .	123

EDWARD IRVING:
MAN, PREACHER, PROPHET

CHAPTER I

Edward Irving's Period and the Impending Changes. Heredity. Preparatory Years.

Looking backward from the twentieth century through the changes wrought by the nineteenth, one sees that that tremendous cycle introduced changes in material things that virtually created a new earth, so that if it were possible to transport a man of to-day back a hundred years, the world he found would seem to him utterly alien and barren of comfort. Great as have been the changes wrought in the external world by that century, changes in creeds and moral standards are no less marked, and while building upon material lines, there has been what has seemed a crumbling along so-called religious lines. Only yesterday, as it were, most men who believed anything spiritual and accepted any creed, took it for granted that whatever they personally believed or whatever creed had won their adherence, contained all that there was of truth in the world, and looking down from his particular vantage ground, considered all men on any other level either heathen or heretic.

But into the spiritual world as into the material, changes or growth that no man could measure were coming. One of old, wiser than men had said, "The kingdom of God cometh not with observation." True as in His own age when His own race could not receive the truth that a little child born in a stable might become greater than any Cæsar ever reigning in imperial Rome, and introduce changes that should indeed "turn the world upside down," the men who believed in the nineteenth century could not easily receive the thought that whatever of dogma or creed might have to go down in the coming struggle between Science and Religion, growth, brotherhood, applied Christianity, and the incoming of the Kingdom of God on earth lay surely in advance along the lines that Christianity and Science were each to travel toward the future. Certain men were to make great discoveries and inventions; other men just as great were to readjust lines of Christian thinking and serving. The successful inventors and discoverers were to be crowned with honors and with wealth. The men who "followed the gleam" of Truth and "blazed" the path toward spiritual freedom and assured faith were often to be crowned as had been their Master, with thorns, and to die

MAN, PREACHER, PROPHET

before they saw the result of their labors. Some of them indeed—Wesley, Maurice, Newman, Bushnell, Martineau,—lived to see the obloquy cast upon their early labors changed to praise. One however who did perhaps as much as, if not more than, any other, save Wesley, to deepen and broaden Christian thinking, was cast out of his own great church for preferring the Bible as his teacher to the elaborate creed of his church, and died brokenhearted in his prime, leaving a name so obscured by the unjust judgment of his brethren in the church and the sad misunderstanding of one great man whom he had most faithfully loved and served that even to-day, seventy-five years after his death, he is utterly misunderstood by the great majority of men, and still inherits the promise, "Blessed are ye when men shall revile you and shall cast out your name as evil for my sake."

But it seems to the writer of this sketch that whatever the world may owe to Edward Irving, she certainly in justice to herself needs to add to her list of resplendent names the name of the man who stood in the van in the defense of Christian sincerity, brotherhood and absolute loyalty to all the truth he saw.

Born in 1792, Edward Irving was the son of Gavin and Mary Lowther Irving. His father was a man of the ordinary Scottish mold, energetic, reserved, successful and a devout Presbyterian. His mother, Huguenot by descent, was an unusual woman. To her, her children owed the peculiar charm of person and manner that distinguished them. To his latest day Edward held her in the highest veneration. The family was prosperous, most comfortably situated, and able to educate their eight children on the best lines then common. Looking at the future through ordinary eyes, one could see nothing of the tremendous changes just ahead for all men. True, the American Revolution had opened a new world to the poor and discontented of all lands, and the French Revolution was baptizing a nation just across the channel in the blood of some of its noblest as well as in that of some of its vilest citizens; but the world as a whole was going on as of old, and no one foresaw the evil days, as they would have termed them, that were to come to all religious and thoughtful men in Protestant lands. Edward Irving, who was destined to become known as one of the greatest actors on the theological stage and in many minds the most subversive of religious teachers, was unusual even from his boyhood. Thoughtful and intellectual beyond his mates, he was also as noted in athletic lines as in mental superiority. One illustration of his religious nature even in boyhood, remains. Before he was twelve he walked Sundays to a church six miles distant with the older men of the parish to listen to a spiritual preacher, as the minister of their own parish, holding a life tenure of his office, could not be deposed, despite his unworthiness.

Irving's native town, Annan, was at that time the seat of one of the most noted schools in Scotland—Annan Academy. Its dominie, Adam Hope, was famous in all the universities for his success in fitting men for college. Poor as was Scotland in those days in material things, she was rich in men of brains and general ability; and Adam Hope's graduates, as capable as their brethren generally, were more fortunate than many in the high cultivation they won from him. Edward Irving and Thomas Carlyle were indeed his most famous graduates, but all over Scotland and India were men bearing his stamp who were making their mark wherever they were. Edward Irving graduated at thirteen, easily carrying away the honors even from his own elder brother, as well he might if it is true, as was asserted, that within a week he mastered five books of Euclid, and in half that time went joyously through six books of Homer. Always passionately fond of poetry, one can imagine what the opening joys of those six books must have meant to him.

Entering the University of Edinburgh at thirteen, there he also carried off the honors.

At that period no profession ranked higher in the estimation of the devout Scotch, nor even of those who sought simply social recognition, than that of minister of the gospel; and to Edward Irving, the son of a rigid Presbyterian father, and of a Huguenot mother whose family had endured exile for their faith, the ministry was the one calling possible. His first year after leaving the University was spent in theological study in Edinburgh. After the first year, the custom of the times made it possible for the theological student to pursue his studies where he chose, simply requiring his return for his examinations.

CHAPTER II

Teaching. Jean Baillie Welsh. Isabella Martin. Thomas Carlyle.

A year after his graduation Irving secured a position as master in the school at Haddington through the influence of Professor Leslie, professor of mathematics in Edinburgh, who equally with Prof. Cristison in the Humanities, as it was called, expected Irving to distinguish himself along his own special line. Although still but a boy, in reality Irving had all the moral dignity of a mature man and was already distinguished in his bearing and in his personal appearance. Wherever he went all his life long, he won without effort the friendship and admiration of the noblest whom he met. It was one of his peculiarities that he could not be forgotten either by peasant or by man of the world.

At Haddington, as elsewhere, he made hosts of friends, but in one family he was most warmly welcomed. Dr. John Welsh, the notable doctor of the countryside, opened his home and his heart to young Irving, and at once made him the tutor of his only child, little Jean, whose life was to be so pathetically influenced later by the friendship thus formed. An only child, always delicate and fragile, she possessed a brain of remarkable power, and a heart as loyal as it was strong and tender. She was to prove in some respects a woman to be greatly pitied, through the unwisdom of some and the cruel desire for exploitation on the part of others. But she was to be greatly loved by two of the greatest men of her period in Scotland, and to render incalculable service to one at least of the two. In some respects no woman has deserved more of her peers and received less. The writer of this article will be glad if in some degree she may present her with something of justice in her estimate formed after the most careful study. In Carlyle's "Reminiscences" he gives a story told to him by Jean Welsh about her father; that riding home one day from his long round of visits, Dr. Welsh spied a little bird with broken wings, left by the careless hunter who had shot it, to die by the roadside from whence it could not remove itself. Causing his groom to dismount and lift the bird gently, the Doctor held it tenderly in one hand until he had reached his own home; then dismounting with as little jar to the bird as possible, he carried it into his office, set its broken wings deftly, placed it in a cage where he personally attended to its wants until it was able to fly. Then, opening the door of its cage, he had the pleasure of seeing a strong and happy bird fly gayly back to its native haunts. Might not a man so considerate of a wounded bird, claim something of justice at least for the memory of the little daughter he loved so much, who was to make so brave a struggle in her later days and whose memory at least was to be sadly marred by careless hunters?

Remaining in Haddington two years, Irving was then promoted to a more important post in the town of Kirkcaldy. There it was his fortune to remain seven years, finishing during that time his theological studies, forming friendships that were to last through life, and as always in all possible ways serving all whom he met. Here another home opened to him— the manse of Kirkcaldy. The minister in the manse, Rev. Dr. Martin, was a devout, strong man, and the family a very religious one. As many another young man impulsive and honest-hearted has done, thrown much into the society of cordial young ladies, the young dominie after awhile imagined himself in love with one of the daughters of the manse, Isabella Martin, and forthwith bound himself fast by one of those Scottish engagements harder far to break in those days than many an actual marriage to-day.

Here too in Kirkcaldy he met another friend, Thomas Carlyle, to whom he was to render inestimable service and to receive from him after his own death, despite a friendship that time could not destroy, the "Eulogy" which perhaps more than anything else has caused literary men to rate Irving as a religious fanatic, even to the point of madness. They met on this wise: Irving's rule as a teacher, while most inspiring to boys who cared to learn, seemed to some of the parents of some of his dullards too strenuous; they sent for Thomas Carlyle, a later graduate of the same great academy in Annan where Irving had won his first honors. Carlyle of course, born pessimist, expected to be received as a rival, but to his great surprise Irving met him and to his astonished rival said with outstretched hand and beaming smile, "You are coming to Kirkcaldy. Two men of Annan must not be strangers in Fife. You must make my house your home and I will help you to look over the field"; which he did so effectively that he materially advanced the fortunes of the new dominie. Thenceforward till the end he was to Carlyle—to quote from the latter—"the freest, brotherliest, bravest human soul mine ever came in contact with. I call him, on the whole, the best man I have ever (after hard trial enough) found in this world or now hope to find." The records that remain prove beyond question that through Irving's influence on others and his personal advice to Carlyle, the latter won his full entrance into literature and was thus made known to the world.

The following are illustrative extracts from Irving's letters later to Carlyle:—

"Known you must be before you can be employed. Known you will not be for a winning, attaching, accommodating man, but for an original, commanding, and rather self-willed man. Now establish this last character, and you take a far higher grade than any other. How are you to establish it? Just by bringing yourself before the public as you are. First find vent for your notions. Get them tongue; upon every subject get them tongue, not upon law alone. You cannot at present get them either utterance or audience by ordinary converse. Your utterance is not the most favorable. It convinces, but does not persuade; and it is only a very few (I can claim place for myself) that it fascinates. Your audience is worse. They are generally (I exclude myself) unphilosophical, unthinking drivelers who lie in wait to catch you in your words, and who give you little justice, or even mercy, in the rencounter. Therefore, my dear friend, some other way is to be sought for. Now pause, if you be not convinced of this conclusion. If you be, we shall proceed. If you be not, read again, and you will see it just, and as such admit it. Now what way is to be sought for? I know no other than the press. You have not the pulpit as I have, and where perhaps I have the advantage. You have not good and influential society. I know nothing but the press for your purpose. None are so good as these two, the *Edinburgh Review* and *Blackwood's Magazine*. Do not steal away and say, 'The one I am not fit for, the other I am not willing for.' Both pleas I refuse. The *Edinburgh Review* you are perfectly fit for; not yet upon law, but upon any work of mathematics, physics, general literature, history, and politics, you are as ripe as the average of their writers. *Blackwood's Magazine* presents bad company, I confess; but it also furnishes a good field for fugitive writing, and good introductions to society on one side of the question. This last advice, I confess, is against my conscience, and I am inclined to blot it out; for did I not rest satisfied that you were to use your pen for your conscience, I would never ask you to use it for your living."

"I like the tone of your last letter; for, remember, I read your very tones and gestures, at this distance of place, through your letter, though it be not the most diaphanous of bodies."

"You live too much in an ideal world, and

MAN, PREACHER, PROPHET 13

you are likely to be punished for it by an unfitness for practical life. It is not your fault but the misfortune of your circumstance as it has been in a less degree of my own. This situation will be more a remedy for that than if you were to go back to Edinburgh. Try your hand with the respectable illiterate men of middle life, as I am doing at present, and perhaps in their honesty and hearty kindness you may be taught to forget and perhaps to undervalue the splendors, and envies and competitions of men of literature. I think you have within you the ability to rear the pillars of your own immortality, and, what is more, of your own happiness, from the basis of any level in life. All that is valuable of the literary caste you have in their writings. Their conversations, I am told, are full of jealousy and reserve, or, perhaps to cover that reserve, of trifling."

In addition to such practical written advice, Irving exerted his personal influence among his own friends in Carlyle's behalf, and welcoming him as a brother, into his own London home as in the old Kirkcaldy days, gladly sheltered him there till he found employment that enabled him to support himself comfortably elsewhere.

How on Irving's exit from the world, Carlyle doubtless unintentionally, but none the less effectively and we regret to add, unjustly, helped to close the door and seal it for a time, behind his vanishing friend, is easily proven by part of the strange "Eulogium," written immediately after Irving's death.

CHAPTER III

Prolonged Probationing. Considers Mission Work. Jean Welsh Reappears. Call to Assist Dr. Chalmers. Terrible Conditions in Glasgow. Applied Christianity Conquers.

Not an easy matter even to-day, in those earlier years Scottish pulpits were harder still to win. Once installed, a minister could not be deposed save for some flagrant sin. Mere drunkenness was no disability, and so long as three persons would listen to a man's preaching, he could defy the whole parish to oust him. Hence positions were as a rule lifelong and a vacancy could not be filled save by a so-called Patron, usually the richest and often by no means the godliest man in the parish. Hence it easily follows that while there were many men of profound piety in the Scottish pulpits, there were some also absolutely unfitted to preach the gospel, and many a most worthy candidate died without securing a pastorate.

Irving, waiting for years for a call that did not come, studied carefully what he believed to be needed in a Christian minister. These years of waiting, hard as they were, proved in his case but the cutting of a diamond that was to shine with resplendent luster. His voice, naturally flexible and musical, was subjected to the most thorough cultivation. Always passionately fond of Nature, he spent long hours on the moors and hills of the countryside, passing often by the lonely graves of Scottish martyrs who from their dust breathed inspiration to his soul, and in these long rambles giving to his voice the most perfect training till he was so thoroughly its master that he could speak as in a whisper audible all over a church, or fill the church as with the tones of a noble organ. During his silent years he had given himself to a careful study of the effects produced by other preachers, noting all their failures and by degrees creating in his own mind an ideal preacher. He destroyed all his written sermons and set himself to preach as from the depths of his own soul what he honestly believed to be God's message to men.

Finally, after four years of waiting had passed since he had completed his theological studies, he decided that there was no place for him in his own country to preach the gospel, and set himself to prepare for the foreign field. What his ideals about missionary work were, we shall learn later. Virtually breaking with his past and ceasing his efforts to find an opening into a pulpit he went back to

Edinburgh for one more term of study to prepare himself for the work he now looked forward to.

There he again met Jean Baillie Welsh, now a most charming woman of eighteen, softened by the suffering her father's recent death had caused her. Irving too had loved her father, and nothing was more natural than that the two should be often thrown together;—nothing also more inevitable than that two so alike mentally and socially and perhaps at that time spiritually, should be drawn very close to each other before either realized the danger in which Irving as an engaged man, and moreover a man who if he became a missionary after his own ideal must not marry, found himself. However, enough passed between them for each to understand the new joy that had come into their lives. Jean Welsh went home. Irving, supposing himself defeated in his own country, and desiring time to meet and quiet the new tumult that had arisen in his heart, buried himself for some weeks in the wilds of remotest Ireland where no mails could reach him.

During his stay in Edinburgh he had preached one day for a friend and learned later that Dr. Chalmers, then Scotland's foremost preacher, had been in his audience. As, however, Chalmers did not seek to meet Irving, the fact was dismissed with hardly a passing thought. On his return from Ireland, however, Irving was astonished to find a letter from Dr. Chalmers awaiting him, inviting him to become his associate in a new work he was about to begin in Glasgow. At the head of a wealthy congregation and easily the leader in the great Presbyterian church, Chalmers, realizing the political and religious dangers of the day, had resigned the pulpit of the powerful Tron church and turned aside to work among the poorest of his countrymen. It was a time of great political peril. The French Revolution lay but a few years behind, and in Great Britain want and suffering among the poor were creating dangers not unlike those that had set the poor against the rich in France. In Great Britain the fear was so great that in many of the cities the upper classes had formed themselves into military organizations, ready to defend themselves at a moment's notice. More than once even in Glasgow before sunrise the signal went around to those organized for the defense of the city to come with all speed to the appointed rendezvous. The hand of the rich was on their guns, that of the starving poor quivering to be at the gunners' throats. One careless shot, one frenzied murder, and the days of "The Terror" might have been re-lived in Glasgow or in Manchester. And every man knew it and

MAN, PREACHER, PROPHET 19

walked as on the verge of a volcano that might at any moment burst asunder.

Chalmers saw all this and realized that whatever might be true of other parts of the kingdom, the gospel and the gospel alone would save the masses of hungry people in Scotland and he undertook a work that few believed feasible—that of helping them to wait in patience, if in suffering, for better days. To assist him in this work he called to Irving who responded to the call and gave the interview desired. He frankly told Dr. Chalmers that while he would gladly work with him with all his heart, Chalmers must not be surprised if his people would not receive him. "If they listen to me," he said with profound humility, "they will be the first people I have found that would."

The work was at once begun. With the ability of a skilled general rather than that of a preacher, Chalmers organized the whole of Glasgow into districts, established schools for the thousands of neglected children roaming the streets, and with Irving and a body of teachers and other assistants, began his work. Knowing that the worst thing in the world for a Scotchman was pauperism, Sundays or week-days Dr. Chalmers from the beginning fell back upon the old Scottish method of having a "Plate" placed at the door of the church in which his hearers might deposit whatever they pleased. This had been the custom in their old home churches and it at once appealed to the tenderest memories as well as to the self-respect even of the poorest. To the astonishment of the city at large, from the beginning Chalmers' church supported itself and continued to do so for some years after his death. It not only supported itself—the poor in the city generally began to respect themselves, and the time speedily came when all dangers of an uprising had passed.

In the interval, however, Irving had gone about his work somewhat differently from the methods of Dr. Chalmers, even while loyally supporting him. Brotherly from boyhood his heart went out intensely toward these suffering people and wherever he went among them he carried not only the strange salutation he always used among his people, "The blessing of the Lord be upon this house," but he carried a heart open to share all their sorrows and whatever else he had he gave to them. Ordinarily he had little money, but a legacy of a few hundred dollars coming to him, he at once turned it into shillings and sixpences with which he helped to supply many a scanty table. Many stories are told of his life among that people, and while not prefiguring his future eloquence, they prove to the utmost his wealth of human sympathy and his ability in helping the poor and sorrowing Godward.

After two years of service there, however, he began to realize that this was not to be his permanent work—that another could do the work that he was doing and that fuller service somewhere was calling to him. To his surprise, however, the call came not from India or Africa, but from London.

CHAPTER IV

Call to London. Strange Acceptance. Unparalleled Success.

The pulpit of the Scotch Caledonian chapel in London, a church built originally for the use of the orphans of dead Presbyterian soldiers and sailors, was vacant and some unknown person recommended Irving and he was called to consider the position. There were, however, two requirements that he would have to meet. As most of the orphans were of Highland parentage, one service each Sunday was to be wholly in Gaelic—a language about as easy to master as Chinese. In addition it was imperative that every Scottish church should be able to assure its minister a proper livelihood and at that time that chapel, reduced to a membership of fifty, could not possibly offer this; but Irving, knowing these difficulties, went up and preached for them and made a deep impression. Finding that they really desired his services he wrote the trustees a letter quite as original as his statement to Dr. Chalmers about himself. He said in substance that "in case he should come among them he would deem it an honor and privilege if he might not only support himself but assist in the general support of the church." As he could not be ordained without the consent of the presbytery, and that would depend on the amount of income assured him, he calmly adds that "if it was decided that they wished him to come, he would come, ordination or no ordination, letting that take care of itself later," and thus he gives the first glimpse of his later independence of church polity.

But the Duke of York, one of the patrons of the church, heard him preach, and all difficulties were thereafter speedily adjusted; and he went up to London to his insignificant little church and poor people with a joy impossible for many modern candidates to understand. Neither he nor his people felt the slightest foreshadowing of the wondrous changes that lay but a few months in advance. He began his work as he had begun in Glasgow, giving to it his whole heart and soul. But the privacy he so lamented later was to last but a little while.

Irving, at this time twenty-nine years old, was as striking in personal appearance as he was talented and strangely magnetic. During the years of his long waiting for a pulpit he had striven in every possible way to develop all his spiritual strength and all possible aids to his power as a preacher. Eloquent, however, as was his preaching, all who have heard him declare that his prayers were absolutely indescribable. "He seems to forget himself," said one, "and his audience, and to stand simply in God's own presence speaking to Him as a son to his own father and asking what he knows the father will surely give him, and somehow he lifts his people up into his own spirit." He was about six feet four inches in height and of a form and bearing that so attracted passing strangers that many a one turned to gaze on him as he passed on the street. His memory was stored not only with the Bible and the fathers of the church, but with Shakespeare, Ossian and all the poets of the day, whom he used freely, interpreting them all through his own irresistible tones, uttered in the manner of one of the old prophets. It is said that his pulpit style never changed, though his audience certainly did.

His chapel was stirred to its center and the news that a young Scotchman of unusual power had come to London soon reached some of his compatriots who, clannish as are all Scotchmen, hastened to hear him,—among them Wilkie the painter, Cunningham the poet, and Sir James Mackintosh, distinguished alike as scholar, jurist and author.

One Sunday Sir James Mackintosh heard Irving pray for a family of children who had lost not only their parents lately in the communion of the church, but also their means of support. Irving spoke of them to God as now dependent alone "on His Fatherhood," and he assumed all that that meant to his own high spiritual sense. The words or the tones or the peculiar union with God that Irving's prayer always suggested, so impressed Sir James, that meeting Canning, the then prime minister of England the next day, he told him about Irving, his eloquence, and above all, the uplifting power of his prayers. The next Sunday, Canning himself was one of Irving's hearers. Soon after a discussion arose in the House of Commons on the revenues of the church, and the necessity that great talent should always be well paid. It suited Canning to state that from his personal knowledge this was not always the case; that in a poor little chapel in London he had lately listened to a young preacher trained in a denomination whose churches were most poorly endowed and preaching in one of that church's outlying dependencies with no endowment at all, preach the most eloquent sermon that he had ever listened to. That was sufficient. Given Irving's power to hold his hearers, there could henceforth be no more privacy for him and his poor little chapel, whose membership, however, had already been doubled.

At once his chapel was crowded to its utmost limits. The most famous people in London packed it to the doors every Sunday. The pressure was so great that tickets for outsiders for admission had to be secured six weeks in advance, and not a foot of standing room was vacant. To prevent serious accidents, the street facing the chapel was divided by ropes, carriages passing up one side, and down on the other. The reviews of the day were crowded with criticisms of his manner and style of preaching, no one, however, denying his power. Hazlitt, the noted critic, makes him the theme of some of his most trenchant essays, seeming to think it incredible that a preacher should be equally at home in the Bible and in Shakespeare, while all who heard him testified to his unusual power. His sermons were of great length, never less than two hours, sometimes three hours in duration. An aged man who had regularly listened to him while himself a student in London, said to the writer: "I have never known any one else who possessed Irving's power. He read the Scriptures as one reading a direct message from God. He prayed as one who speaks with God. When he began to preach one forgot everything but the message he was listening to. Absolute silence reigned and one was unconscious of the flight of time. When he ceased speaking one became conscious that not only himself but every person in the church was bending forward as if afraid of losing a word, and a deep sigh not of weariness, but of mental exaltation was breathed from all as they sat again erect in their seats."

CHAPTER V

Decision as to Marriage. Comments by Carlyle and Mrs. Oliphant. Marriage to Miss Martin. Birth of Little Edward. Death of the Child and its Remarkable Effect on Mr. Irving. Journal Letter "To Comfort Little Edward's Mother." Perfected Union.

Finally assured that he had at last found his place and work, Irving realized that he must now settle the question of his future home life. He had continued his correspondence with Miss Welsh. Of his engagement to Miss Martin and his unforeseen love for herself she had learned. She had declared that she could not listen to him while he was engaged to another. Miss Martin of course had known how things were going, for it was impossible for one of Irving's candor to continue to profess sentiments that had materially changed. Passing by the statements of others concerning this situation, painful to all concerned, and quoting only Carlyle's suggestions in the "Reminiscences," edited by Professor Norton, we learn that there were at one time (before 1821), "on Irving's own part some movements of negotiation over to Kirkcaldy for *release* there, and of hinted hope toward Haddington. . . . And something (as I used to gather long afterwards) might have come of it, had not Kirkcaldy been so peremptory, and stood by its bond (as spoken or as written), 'Bond or utter Ruin, Sir!'—upon which Irving had honorably submitted and resigned himself."

Mrs. Oliphant, in an article in *Macmillan's Magazine*, written after the death of her friend, Mrs. Carlyle, referring to the affair between Mr. Irving and Miss Welsh as in any manner indicated by Mrs. Carlyle in her later days, sums up in this manner: "There were some points about which she was naturally and gracefully reticent—about her own love, and the preference which gradually swept Irving out of her girlish fancy if he had ever been fully established there, a point on which she left her hearer in doubt. But there was another sentiment gradually developed in the tale which gave the said hearer a gleam of amusement unintended by the narrator, one of those sidelights of self-revelation which even the keenest and clearest intelligence lets slip—which was her perfectly genuine feminine dislike of the woman who replaced her in Irving's life. . . . This dislike looked to me nothing more than the very natural and almost universal feminine objection to the woman who has consoled even a rejected lover. The only wonder was that she did not herself . . . see the humor of it."

These two extracts, we think, quite sustain the assertion that, like many another young man who perfectly honest and true-hearted has become engaged in his early twenties but later finds himself more deeply interested in a later friend, Edward Irving found himself in the painful position of wishing to seek a release from a woman to whom he had been long engaged. To many noble women it must seem quite incomprehensible that he was not at once released, no matter at what cost of pain and disappointment. But to understand the attitude of Dr. Martin and his daughter, it must be clearly understood that an engagement openly announced and adhered to for years was considered in those days, in Scotland, quite as sacred and binding as a genuine marriage bond is in many lands to-day. Doubtless they felt almost as keenly hurt as if, after the marriage service, Edward Irving had asked to be released. Only one thing is certain to-day, that to their decision, welcome or unwelcome as it may have been at the time, Edward Irving owed the truest happiness and the most perfect fellowship of his later years; while to Thomas Carlyle and Jean Baillie Welsh came a future which to each was doubtless the highest consummation of their lives.

Fortunately no details remain of any correspondence on the subject that might by accident have fallen into the hands of some writer willing to violate the secrets of the dead. No one at all familiar with the life of Isabella Martin during the years subsequent to her marriage to Edward Irving, can doubt that if God ever provided a devoted and beloved wife who was also a most efficient "help-meet" for all the duties and cares and sorrows that crowded Edward Irving's remaining years, His hand certainly united this remarkable couple. And not only in their case but in many another since the world began, people who have at one time earnestly desired to marry each other often find as time goes on that the Providence or fate, whichever they may choose to call it, that thwarted their once dearest hopes, planned for them more tenderly than in their unwisdom they had planned for themselves.

On the 13th of October, 1823, Edward Irving and Isabella Martin were married in the old manse at Kirkcaldy by the venerable grandfather of the bride and at once departed on their brief wedding journey, duly returning to London and beginning the work that was to be so varied, so heavy, and till violently attacked, so pre-eminently useful.

It seems a little strange to note that but for Mrs. Oliphant's noble "Life of Edward Irving," his memory must greatly have faded from the minds of men, as, until her "Life" was published, nearly thirty years after his death, only brief and often imperfect sketches of the real man had appeared, although the British magazines for a long time contained sketches of him that though most interesting, were ephemeral.

In the faithful execution of her labor of love she was greatly assisted by Mrs. Irving's sister (Mrs. Irving herself having died many years previous), who was very anxious that a correct Life of Irving should be published and gladly furnished all the information in her power, including Irving's letter "To Comfort Little Edward's Mother," and his other letters to his wife. Irving's children and other personal friends also contributed whatever information they possessed, and the biography became, if somewhat lengthy, a mine of valuable information concerning the man and the preacher, although of course it could not foretell imminent changes that were to give permanent value to some of his teachings. She also made in this work the personal acquaintance of Thomas Carlyle and his wife, and to Mrs. Carlyle she owed much valuable information as to the facts of Irving's early manhood. Mrs. Oliphant seems to have been as just and appreciative to the Carlyles as she was to Edward Irving, and in her own Autobiography and Letters she has given some exquisite glimpses of their domestic life.

Once more busy as preacher, pastor and author, Edward Irving was valiantly striving to throw his whole soul into his work; but an experience that lay before him proved to himself as it now reveals to us, the fact that, as has more than once been the case with others, he was fighting a foe that would have sadly hampered him but for God's chastening hand. In mid-summer, 1824, a new current of joy came into his life when his first child was born— the little Edward, that "glorious bud of being," as Irving styled him who so filled his father's heart with overflowing delight as to excite some of Carlyle's most characteristic comments.

In the autumn of 1825 the child died of whooping cough at his mother's old home in the manse of Kirkcaldy, whither they had gone for the child's health and also for the sake of its mother who was in delicate health. Unable to return with her husband when he went back to his church in London, Irving wrote her a "Journal,"—"To Comfort Little Edward's Mother," covering a space of several weeks and certainly unique among men's love-letters to their wives. In it he speaks with singular sincerity, yet delicately, of the divisions that had existed between them, assuming all the blame. He seems to have believed the death of little Edward, by the depth of its pain to them and the awakening of his conscience, meant by God to bring them into a perfect union and a fellowship in love and service that nothing henceforth would be able to break. These letters are filled with the tenderest expressions of love and gratitude to God for the gift of such a wife, and the full assurance of their future reunion with the child of their love. This journal covers eighty closely printed pages in Mrs. Oliphant's "Life of Irving," and really gives the key-note to all their future life.

To quote from Mrs. Oliphant: "This journal perhaps has no parallel in modern days. A picture so minute, yet so broad, a self-revelation so entire—a witness so wonderful of that household love, deepened by mutual suffering and sorrow, which so far transcends in its gravity and soberness the voluble passions of youth, has never, so far as I am aware, been given to the world. . . . Few men or heroes have been laid in their graves with such a memorial as envelops the baby name of little Edward, and I think few wives will read this record without envying Isabella Irving

MAN, PREACHER, PROPHET 35

that hour of her anguish and consolation."

Unique as a masterpiece of intellectual and spiritual communion with a wife whom he had come to love with all his heart, the Journal glows with the enthusiastic delight of a strong man's soul in the beauties of nature as he treads the hills and valleys of Scotland on his way back to London, describes alike sympathetically, the cottages of the poor where he spends nights in passing, and the mansions of the rich, shares his every thought of prayer and of rejoicing in God with her, even makes his dreams vivid to her, bears her with him as he repasses the scenes they have visited with their little vanished boy, shares his hours of depression and of exaltation with her, as if she were in truth a part of his own soul, and finally in utter humility shows her his consciousness of weakness in the past as well as his strength in the present to which God has lifted them with hands close-clasped, that shall never again be sundered. We quote some of the more personal parts of the Journal premising as we do so that while we believe that as a rule such intimate revelations should be sacred to the one to whom they are written, we also believe that there are times when their truest lessons may rightfully be carefully studied by others in kindred needs. Both Irving and his wife, we believe, to-day would willingly share with others the full knowledge of whatever depths of pain God led them through to peace and perfect fellowship, if by that sharing, others might be warned, comforted and strengthened. Moreover, it is only by realizing the depths of Irving's nature as husband and father in this sad but uplifting experience as well as by studying him carefully as he defends himself later before the London Presbytery, that one can truly understand and appreciate the sincere, tender soul of the man and the logical, consistent course of the faithful Minister of Jesus Christ. We give in their sequence, though with much abbreviation, some of these intimate communings.

"Nov. 7th. Though wearied, my dearest Isabella, with a day of much activity, and afterward with an exposition, and now with much discourse and discussion to James P. whom I like exceedingly, and William Hamilton, all concerning the subordination of the sensual and visible, and the intellectual or knowable to the spiritual or redeemable, I do now sit down with true spiritual delight to commune with my soul's sweet mate. Yea, hath not the Lord made us for one another, and by His providence united us to one another, against many fiery trials and terrible delusions of Satan? And, as you yourself observed, has He not over again wedded us, far more closely than in any joy, by our late tribulation, and the burial of our lovely Edward, our holy first born, who gave up the ghost in order to make his father and mother one, and expiate the discords and divisions of their souls? Dear spirit, thou dearest spirit which doth tenant heaven, this is the mystery of thy burial on the wedding day of thy parents, to make them forever one. Oh, and thou shalt be sanctified, God blessing, by such a concord and harmony of soul as hath not often blessed the earth since Eden was forfeited by sin. My wife, this is not poetry, this is not imagination, which I write: it is truth that lovely Edward hath been the sweet offering of peace between us forever; and so, when we meet in heaven, he shall be as the priest who joined us—the child of months being one hundred years old. Let my dear wife be comforted by these thoughts of her true love. I found much sweet meditation upon my bed last night, and when I awoke in the morning, He was with me, and I had much countenance of the Lord in my secret devotions. . . . Farewell, dear Isabella. You cannot have so much pleasure in reading these as I have in writing them. The blessing of the Lord be with my babe"—(the little Margaret) "My tender babe. The blessing of the

Lord be with her mother,—her tempted but victorious mother.

"Nov. 9th. I wish to read the Sabbath lessons, at least in the Hebrew. . . . It would perhaps be an entertainment to your heart to accompany me, that we do not be divided in this study when we meet again. But I forget that you have the dear babe to watch over; for whom, my dear, let our souls be exercised rather than for the dead.

"Nov. 10th. . . . Our little boy! thou art incorporated with my memory dearly, with my hope thou art incorporated still more dearly. We will come, when our Lord doth call, to thee and to the general assembly of the first born. Oh, Isabella, I exhort thee to be diligent in thy prayers for thee and me!

"Nov. 16th. Dear, lovely Edward, what a sweet tabernacle was that over which thy mother and I wept so sadly! My much beloved child, my much cherished, much beloved child, dwell in the mercies of my God, and the God of thy mother! We will follow thee betimes, God strengthening us for the journey.

"Nov. 21st. May the Lord of His great mercy fill my soul with the fullness of love to my dear wife; that as Christ loved the Church, I may love her, and in like manner manifest with all gracious words my unity of soul with her soul; that we may be one as Thou, our Creator,

MAN, PREACHER, PROPHET 39

didst intend man and woman to be from the beginning."

Thus end our quotations from this rare journal of love, tenderness, pain and overcoming faith. The hand that wrote it and the eyes that dwelt with tender gladness upon it, have been dust for scores of years, but doubtless somewhere among the dearest treasures of the remaining Irving family, still lie in safety these time-colored pages. Strange that perishable paper, far less durable than parchment, should outlast the intensest mortal feelings; but, thank God, we may believe that while these records must also some day crumble into dust, the souls that lived and suffered and overcame, are still but on the threshold of their eternal life and growth and service, going on forever into all the fullness of God's truth, now no longer parted from their once vanished boy.

We believe that no mother of a vanished child can read this Journal-letter without feeling in her heart a strange and unforgetable kinship to the man who wrote it; nor that any wife to whom children have not been given can read it without realizing that it is truly better to have loved and "lost awhile" than to have missed the deepest human loving[1] and that

[1] Although Thomas Carlyle and his wife passed through no such experiences of bereavement, words

even the depth of a sorrow like the Irvings' must become and remain, glorified by the con-

written by each prove that another sorrow, keener if possible than that of the Irvings, became theirs as the years went on, and we deem it as just to their memory, each once so closely associated with Irving, to quote lines that prove their nobility in their loneliness as clearly as Irving proved his in his letter to his wife. We find in Mrs. Carlyle's exquisite "Lines to a Swallow Building under Our Eaves" abundant proof of the pain of childless loneliness, as truly as in Carlyle's reference to her little chair. One stanza of her pathetic poem runs thus:—

"God speed thee, pretty bird; may thy small nest
With little ones all in good time be blessed.
         I love thee much;
For well thou managest that life of thine,
While I; oh, ask not what I do with mine!
         Would I were such!"

Some time after his wife's death Mr. Carlyle wrote: "Her little bit of a first chair, its wee, wee arms, etc., visible to me in the closet at this moment, is still here, and always was; I have looked at it hundreds of times: from of *old,* with many thoughts. No daughter or son of *hers* was to sit there; so it had been appointed us, my Darling. I have no *Book* thousandth part so beautiful as Thou; but these were *our* only 'Children,' and in a true sense, these *were* verily OURS; and will perhaps live some time in the world, after we are both gone; and be of no damage to the poor brute chaos of a world, let us hope! The will of the Supreme shall be accomplished; *Amen.*"

Could there be given a sweeter, yet more plaintive echo from the heart of the home, so full of genius, so thronged by the noblest in the world then living, and yet lacking one of God's supreme gifts, the love and joyousness of little children?

sciousness of the immortality of a love that those only can fully understand who have known it.

The death of their boy seems to have been the one thing needed to lift Edward Irving above all human selfishness and transform him into a minister of God consecrated in every desire and longing only to deliver with absolute loyalty whatever he believed to be God's message to men. Thenceforth, unlimited service, many a conflict, and eventually a broken heart lay before him within the radius of a few short years, but no one reading his life and labors dispassionately can question that he went forth to meet his future as seeing the invisible and caring only for the doing of God's will. Back to their united work a little later went Irving and his wife, thenceforth with perfectly united hearts, but to pass into ever increasing labors, and in a few short years into deepening ecclesiastical clouds.

CHAPTER VI

Growing Influence. New Church in Regent's Square. Peculiar Dedications to Books. Unpopular Missionary Sermon.

Mr. Irving had no time for society as such, yet there was no man outside the highest political positions more prominently before the public in those days than he. His wife wholly adapted herself to his home requirements. Their breakfast table became one of the leading religious centers of London. Around it gathered every morning, representatives of all classes prominent in every line of Christian service, or earnest seekers after truth. For a couple of hours a day Irving gave himself to this method of meeting his fellows. How he managed in the remaining twenty-two hours of the day to accomplish the work he did, is a mystery. His church grew and prospered to such an extent that within two years a new building had to be erected, and one large, commodious and beautiful was built by Irving's exertions in Regent's Square, a much more desirable part of the city. It too was crowded to its utmost capacity and his influence seemed monthly to extend in all directions. On all great occasions he was prominent in his own denomination and in much demand elsewhere. His popularity constantly increased and he seemed one of the strongest and most inspired of preachers. He spoke as one of the old prophets—more and more the crowds clamored to hear him. Wherever he went on the briefest notice congregations gathered too large for the churches to hold; but such was the power of his well-trained voice that even out of doors on the outskirts of crowds of ten or twelve thousand, he was clearly heard and without apparent effort.

Walking as he was, as seeing the invisible, it was not long before he ran straight against the visible and tangible. As a rule, prudent writers preface their books so as to attract the interest and not to arouse in advance the criticism of their readers. But Irving spoke as plainly of his motive in writing his books as he did courageously of the subject in the books themselves; and the preface to his first book, "Orations and Arguments for Judgment to Come" (1823), fell like a bomb into the ranks of his clerical brethren. To quote from it, he says: "It hath appeared to the Author of this book, from more than ten years' meditation upon the subject, that the chief obstacle to the progress of divine truth over the minds of men, is the want of its being properly presented to them. This ignorance, in both the higher and lower orders, of Religion as a discerner of the thoughts and intentions of the heart, is not so much due to the want of inquisitiveness on their part, as to the want of a sedulous and skillful ministry on the part of them to whom this ministry is entrusted. To this end they must discover new vehicles for conveying the truth as it is in Jesus, into the minds of the people, poetical, historical, scientific, political and sentimental vehicles. They prepare men for teaching gypsies, for teaching bargemen, for teaching miners; men who understand their ways of conceiving and estimating truth; why not train ourselves for teaching imaginative and political men, and legal men, and medical men? And, having got the key to their several chambers of delusion and resistance, why not enter in and debate the matter with their souls? Then shall they be left without excuse; meanwhile, I think, we ministers are without excuse."

Accustomed still more in those days than in these to hold themselves at liberty to criticise instead of to be criticised, one can easily imagine the effect of such words upon ministers at large. To some it came as a clarion call to deeper consecration and more perfect work; in others it aroused the fighting blood and prepared the way for union against

Irving later. That book, as did all his books, had a large sale, and more and more men's eyes were fixed upon its author. The next event that placed him, if not in antagonism to his brethren, in seeming criticism of their methods for Christian service, came in a missionary sermon preached before the London Missionary Society in 1824.

From the beginning of modern missions, no country had been more deeply interested in them nor contributed more largely to them both in men and money, in proportion to her ability, than Scotland. It was an interest deeply seated in the hearts of all Scottish Christians, and no efforts were spared to win success. The annual preachers before the assemblies were chosen from their most talented men, and the man selected had reason to believe himself alike honored and trusted by his brethren. Of course the work could not be carried on without funds; and the larger the contributions secured, the more effectively could the work be carried forward. Irving at that time seemed second only to Chalmers in the ranks of their preachers, and the sermon he was invited to give was anticipated with enthusiasm both as an opportunity for hearing the man at his best and for securing a large contribution. But to those trusting to his power to fill the coffers of the Society, Irving proved an unknown quantity. We have seen that in earlier days he had seriously considered becoming a missionary, and had formed high ideals of the work, and it was therefore no new subject for his thoughts. Perhaps he himself can best tell the story of the feeling his call to preach the sermon produced in him, and his method of preparing his sermon. He said later: "It seemed to my conscience that I had undertaken a duty full of peril and responsibility, for which I ought to prepare myself with every preparation of the mind and spirit, and thus, not without much prayer to God, and self-devotion, I meditated those things which I delivered in public."

The day for the meeting came. It proved wet and dreary, but long before the hour for the service there were such crowds in the streets that the vast hall was thrown open and was immediately filled to the doors, leaving crowds outside standing in the rain, in the hope that they might later fill vacated places. An hour before the appointed time Irving entered the pulpit and at once addressed himself to his work. His text was Matthew x:5-42. The length of this sermon is not told; but the fact that often his sermons were three hours in length without intermission, and that in this sermon there were two pauses for singing and for rest for the people, proves that it must have been much longer than his usual sermons. It is also told somewhat naïvely that most of the dinners of the Presbyterians in London were spoiled that day, which may not have added in the minds of some to their appreciation of the lessons of the sermon.

But little noted Edward Irving the passing of the hours. He forgot time and place and established Christian methods. He remembered only the Master, the work, and the end; and the thoughts of the perfect Christian service that had been springing up in his own soul during those years of silent consecration, burst forth in a resistless tide upon his astonished hearers. He began after a few preliminaries with a most unexpected statement. "This is the age of expediency," he said, "both in the Church and out of the Church, and all institutions are modeled upon the principles of expediency and carried into effect by the rules of prudence. I remember, in this metropolis, to have heard it uttered and received with great applause in a public meeting, where the heads and leaders of the religious world were present, 'If I were asked what was the first qualification for a missionary, I would say, Prudence; and what the second? Prudence; and what the third? Prudence.' I trembled while I heard, not with indignation but with horror and apprehension, of what the end would be of a spirit which I have since found to be the presiding genius of our activity, the rule of the ascendant. Now, if I read the eleventh chapter of St. Paul's Epistle to the Hebrews, I find that from the time of Abel to the time of Christ, it was by *faith* that the cloud of witnesses witnessed their good confession, and so mightily prevailed, which faith is there defined the substance of things hoped for, the evidence of things not seen; whereas *prudence* or *expediency* is the substance of things present, the evidence of things seen. So that faith and prudence are opposite poles in the soul, the one attracting to it all things spiritual and divine, the other all things sensual and earthly. This expediency hath banished the soul of patriotic eloquence from our senate, the spirit of high equity from our legislation, self-denying wisdom from our philosophy, and of our poetry it hath clipped the angel wing and forced it to creep along the earth. And if we look not to it, it will strangle faith and make void the reality of the things which are not seen, which are the only things that are real and cannot be removed. Money, money, money, is the universal cry. Mammon hath gotten the victory, and may say triumphantly (nay, he may keep silence and the servants of Christ will say it for him), 'Without me ye can do nothing.'"

Thence he proceeded to quote the words of Christ himself in the various gospels, and the records of the men who through all the ages have witnessed noble confessions for the truth in Christ Jesus as they saw it, and gladly given all they had in his service, outlining what he believed to be Christ's will in the preaching of the gospel to those who had not heard it. He certainly believed that he was declaring the real mind of the Lord Jesus Christ in this sermon. But no bombshell straight from the camp of an enemy ever produced greater confusion and anger in the ranks of an army marching against it, than did this plain Gospel re-statement of Christ's missionary teachings produce among nearly all British Christians. Both preacher and congregation have gone their ways into the land of perfect understandings since that remote day; but that sermon is still extant and any reader can easily see in its pages how far Irving's ideals differed from, or agreed with, his Master's. The Scotch are a practical people. Probably most of his hearers had determined the amount of their offering beforehand, and the collection may not have fallen much below that amount; but it certainly did not empty so many pockets as a different line of teaching might have done, and Irving had written another interrogation point in the minds of many of his brethren against his name.

The sermon was at once published, and in a very long preface he dedicates it, of all men, to Samuel T. Coleridge, then little known, and till that time a not highly accredited philosopher. In this introduction Mr. Irving proceeds after this wise further to astonish his own denomination and the world at large. He acknowledges as well understood, the misunderstanding and misrepresentation that Mr. Coleridge had received alike from the church and the world—a misunderstanding he personally had once shared, but asserts that, coming to know him thoroughly, "you have been more profitable to my faith in orthodox doctrine, to my spiritual understanding of the Word of God, and to my right conception of the Christian church, than any or all the men with whom I have entertained friendship or conversation." This was but the beginning of the dedication and it lost nothing in pungency as it proceeded. The years that have followed have shown that Irving, if among the first really to feel and frankly confess the power of Coleridge, was by no means the last or least. No dedication could have been less "prudent," so far as Irving was concerned; but he went his way unheeding what men said or thought, so long as he spoke the truth he saw and felt.

CHAPTER VII

Mr. Hatley Frere. Mr. Henry Drummond and Albury Conferences. Irving Declares Christ the Head of the Church and Creeds Finite.

About this time Mr. Irving became acquainted with a Mr. Hatley Frere, a person who was to exercise much influence over his future by turning his mind into the serious study of prophecy. This man, noted for his learning and his high spirituality, was strongly convinced that in the Bible was foretold the second coming of Christ, near the period in which men were then living. Nothing was more natural than that Irving in his intense belief in revelation, should have felt the strongest desire to test as far as he could the truth of these suggestions; and when Henry Drummond of Albury Park, Surrey, with others, entered upon this study, Irving joined them with deepest interest. Of Henry Drummond Mrs. Oliphant says that he was at once "a religious leader and the patron of religious distress throughout the world; an independent influence and most caustic critic in the British Parliament; a believer in all the mysteries of faith, yet a contemptuous denouncer of everything beyond the shadowy line which he recognized as dividing faith from superstition; the temporal head, in some respects, of a band of religionists, and yet a man in full communion with the busy world, keeping the ear of society, and never out of the fullest tide of life." At his house for years he assembled by special invitation clergymen from all orthodox denominations, as well as laymen who were known to be interested in prophetic studies. There a week was given under the most perfect conditions, to study on these important questions. This would now be called a Retreat. It was then simply the Albury Conference. Out of this Conference, as the result of ostracism in their own churches and their desire for higher spiritual fellowship, later grew the Catholic Apostolic Church, in the formation of which, Irving, then a Presbyterian, had no share and was never a prominent member of it, although for many years after his death its members were, by his countrymen and generally, called Irvingites; probably because he was the most celebrated man who entered its communion after his own church had cast him out. We should say in passing, that this church, noted for the splendor of its ritual but still more for the genuine Christian brotherhood among its members, and its peculiar organization—pat-

terned as much as possible after the order of
the apostolic days—still exists, not given to
proselyting but still calmly confident of its own
call to announce the latest revelation of truth,
and awaiting serenely the speedy coming of the
Kingdom of Christ on earth.

Mr. Irving had always modeled his belief
not merely by human creeds or formulas but
by the New Testament itself, and he began to
find to his surprise that all men did not find
in the New Testament what he found there and
by degrees he became the subject of much
criticism from unexpected sources. The headship of Christ to the church, the oneness in
Him of all believers, including all the baptized
whether adults or infants, and the sure and
speedy coming of His Kingdom were henceforth
to be the basis of all his thinking and of all
his service to the church. To understand the
position in which his belief in the oneness of all
believers placed him, one must glance a moment
at the theological condition of the church in
Irving's day. The Roman, the Episcopal and
the Presbyterian churches each believed themselves the sole repositories of truth and
regarded men outside their own communion either as heretics or heathen. Irving
was a loyal Presbyterian, and had no
thought of stepping outside that fold; but
as the two disciples walking to Emmaus

felt their hearts burn within them as they listened to the words of one a seeming stranger, concerning the crucifixion and the resurrection and felt strangely drawn to Him, so Truth wherever he found it, in the Fathers of his own church, in the anonymous writings of the Jesuits, or anywhere where it seemed to him a message from God, Irving's whole heart responded and he did all in his power to give to others the impression he himself received. His writings became most voluminous. He was in demand everywhere as a preacher on special occasions. His church prospered mightily, and he was multiplying outside means of service for himself and for his people on every side, in many respects not unlike the spirit if not the methods of the present Salvationists.

Engaged in religious work that seems as we read of it, sufficient to have engrossed the lives of two men, he was also a profound student and fared steadily on, eagerly absorbing all books that seemed breathings of new truths or of old truths that he set forth in a new vitality that were to mark new eras in Christian thought and hope long after he had been laid in his grave, hurried thither by the sorrows and storms evoked by his loyalty to the Spirit by which God whispered into his soul, as clearly as in earlier days other "voices" had led Jean d'Arc to the stake.

MAN, PREACHER, PROPHET 55

Believing in the divinity of Christ, Irving accepted Him as the only, though invisible Head of the Church; and as it seemed perfectly right and natural to him, believed that all men everywhere, striving toward the Truth they saw, were His brethren and therefore one in Him. He was still a thorough Presbyterian, but one modeled on the New Testament as he read it, and considering creeds only human interpretations thereof. Had he realized it as he was to later, this was by no means either a "wise" or a "prudent" line of action. Within a very few years we of to-day have seen that some divergence in thinking on lines theological may oust a prominent man from a high position in a church, and Irving, going forward in the simplicity of his faith, was to be one of the most notable examples of the results of standing too literally on the teachings of the New Testament.

As time went on, Irving's influence seemed extending in every direction, his church was growing rapidly, his young men were practising all methods of evangelistic work in the streets and in the dwellings of the poor, and books and pamphlets were coming regularly from his pen, some of them worth reprinting more than thirty years after his death, and he was yearly attending the Albury Conferences. Still there was no cry of heresy in the air.

About this time occurred an accident which was later used by his enemies as a proof of a judgment of God against him. It may be stated that there are few such accidents to-day. Irving had gone to his wife's early home to perform the marriage ceremony between her sister and one of the elders of his church. Invited to preach as he always was when away from his own church, the parish church on Sunday evening was crowded to such an extent that one of the galleries fell beneath the crowd, killing eighteen people and seriously injuring many. Distressing as was this accident at the time, it is doubtful if any one then had the slightest prevision that it would later be quoted solemnly as proof of God's disapproval of Irving; yet it was.

Not caring to cite any of the illustrations that still remain of his eloquence, magnificent as they are, even deprived of the wondrous music of his voice, and the grandeur of his presence, our aim is simply to quote enough of his varied addresses to prove his intense spiritual earnestness, and that but one motive —the glory of God, and power to draw men Godward,—controlled him from the beginning till the ending of his career as a minister of the Lord Jesus Christ. Given a little out of its order here, we subjoin another proof of the simplicity as well as power of his preaching, taken from his sermon at the ordination of the Rev. Hugh McLean, pastor-elect of the Scots' Church, London Wall. In this sermon we find so clearly expressed his own opinions of the duties and experiences of the faithful Christian minister, that we think it wise to quote enough of it to epitomize the sum of his own thinking as to the most desirable results of a faithful ministry,—not wealth, not popularity, nothing that *men* call success measured by an earthly standard. This charge to the young pastor presents the strongest possible refutation to Carlyle's assertion, that, when "fashion went her idle way," Irving, to draw them back again, was capable of resorting to what would have been mere tricks of trade to fill again his diminishing audiences. Fashion's votaries still crowded about him and with an infinite sadness Irving gazed down into their faces, realizing with unutterable pathos how little they were willing or able to take of the infinite treasures God was offering to them. There is no hint of disappointed vanity in this address. It has rather the ring of a man far removed from vanity or from fear, one following closely in the footsteps of a crucified Master, yet sure that he is in full accord with a risen and overcoming Lord, that Lord the hope of whose reappearing was even now filling Irving's heart with ever-growing hope. As always, in this address, Irving blends the practical with the spiritual. He says, in part:

"I speak of those many functions which the new man hath to discharge toward those to whom we are related by other ties than the ministerial, or the pastoral, or the ecclesiastical,—to friends and to acquaintances, to servants, to men in general, and to the society of which thou art a member, and to the civil polity of which thou art a subject. For the present, thou must dwell, like a wayfaring man, in a lodging; but I trust thou wilt soon be master of thine own house, to give thy people a pattern of household government, as Joshua resolved to do, and as every bishop and every elder is required to do. Thou wilt keep hospitality; but *accumulate riches at thy peril.* Oh, if thou grow rich,—oh, if thou shouldst die rich, I will be ashamed of thee. Look at the hard hearts of rich men; look at their self-importance; look at their contempt of Christ; and pray, oh earnestly pray, to be kept from that greatest snare. Thy cloak and thy parchments, brother,—that is, thy decent apparel and thy books,—be these thy riches, and then thou canst speak out against Mammon, and tell those men of thousands and tens of thousands, who thou art surrounded with.

what they should do with their treasures. If thou spare them, God will not spare thee. I give thee it in charge this day, that thou reprove them, and their accumulations sharply. Keep thou hospitality. Shew thou to lordly prelates what the word bishop meaneth. Shew thou to substantial citizens what the word hospitality meaneth; and to all, what faith meaneth. Go thou out as poor a man as thou came in; and let them bury thee when thou diest. And if God should bless thee with a wife and children, put no money in the bank for them, but write prayers in the record of the book of life; be this thy bank of faith; be this thy exchange, even the providence of God; and let the lords of thy treasury be the prophets and the apostles who went before thee. Oh, my brother, be zealous for the good primitive customs of the Church; abjure thou the prudential maxims of this metallic age. Oh, be thou a man far above this world, living by faith in the world to come like one of the elders who have obtained a good report. Be thou of a bold countenance and a lion heart, of a single eye and a simple spirit; otherwise Satan will soon hedge thee in and mow thee up; he will come to thee as a counsellor, but we of the presbytery, whose voice I now speak, are thy counsellors; he will come to thee as a threatener; but who dare meddle with thee, who art Christ's anointed minister; he will come to thee as a flatterer; be thou therefore honest and self-denied. If thou do thy duty, as I trust thou wilt, *thy dearest friends will come to warn thee, and will exceedingly afflict thee by their apprehensions;* but thou art not to be seduced by friends, being this day charged by the whole Church of Christ to be faithful unto Christ, and to no other allegiance. The time is coming, yea, now is, when thou mayest have to testify against wickedness in high places, as did the fathers of the Church; and thou must, and then there will come about thine ears such a hurricane of stormy voices; but, like Elijah, thou must stand in the cleft of the rock till it passeth by. But, if thou hast any floating interest, if thou hast any selfish end, canst thou stand all this, my brother? no, thou wilt shrink and yield every limb of thee. If thou art not ready to die, get ready as fast as thou mayest; for the soldier in the battle who is not ready to die hath two enemies to fight; and if thou be not ready to die for Christ, thou mayest have a hundred; but if thou be ready to die for Christ thou hast but one, who is emphatically the enemy, against whom, that all thine energies may be collected, give this day all interests, all affections, all gains, all talents, all things unto the Lord, and count them but as dung that thou mayest win Christ. What the Lord Jesus, who was followed by a multitude, did say to them indiscriminately, I may well turn round and say to thee His soldier, His captain of a hundred, yet, I trust, to be His captain of a thousand,—'He that would be my disciple must hate father and mother, and sister and wife, and children, and houses and lands, and his own life also,—must take up his cross, and follow me.'"

Remembering that the Lord Jesus had been first followed by multitudes and afterward crucified by some of these same multitudes, Irving, as clear-eyed in his analysis of men and their motives as he was single-hearted in his devotion to Christ, must have known, if man ever did, that mere personal popularity was as transitory and valueless as the beauty of a vanishing soap-bubble. He spoke but his truest, deepest thoughts in this most apostolic charge. Of it Mrs. Oliphant says most truly that "it reads like an ode of the most thrilling and splendid music." It is a gladness to remember that the man so charged walked step by step with Irving through all the coming changes of Irving's remaining years; and, faithful unto death in all the truth God opened to him as to Irving, years after Irving had been called home, he, too, went forward into that perfect knowledge toward which, together, they had bravely striven.

CHAPTER VIII

Cry of Heresy. Religious Awakening in Scotland. Peculiar Manifestations. Baptism of the Holy Spirit. Advent of the "Tongues" in Scotland. First and Second Cases of Healing in Scotland (Presbyterian). Case of Miss Fancourt, in London (Episcopalian). Mr. Irving's Attitude towards These Facts.

In the 17th and 18th centuries, in no Protestant land were the Bible and the Presbyterian Church more deeply enshrined in the hearts of its people than in Scotland. For years in the 17th century the Lowlands had been drenched with the blood of its martyrs and confessors. In his youth and later, Edward Irving's long lonely walks among the hills and moors led often by the graves of martyrs whom Claverhouse and his dragoons had slain. A few miles below Annan lay Wigtown where was still pointed out the spot where on the then dry sands had been placed the stakes to which were bound two women left to die by the incoming tide, who had refused every offer of release if they would "take the test," and

MAN, PREACHER, PROPHET 63

died triumphantly, remembered with grateful reverence even in Irving's day. In short, the Bible and Presbyterianism had been so welded as by fire into the souls of the Scotch, that to them probably more than to any other cause, Scotland owes it long line of heroic and intellectual men, and saintly women. No descendants of that land, exiled to the ends of the earth though they may be, can ever think of the home of their ancestry without a thanksgiving for the influences mental and spiritual that they have inherited from that land, even from its lowliest homes. Naturally among such a people, and in Edward Irving's day, no disgrace could cause more suffering to a sensitive, loyal son of the Presbyterian church, than the charge of heresy—a distress all the deeper probably, in proportion to its injustice, and yet that charge, deadly as it was, was imminent in Irving's path, for suddenly a new sensation burst upon the Presbytery. Like the first gunshot in the early morning that betokens the presence of hostile forces, the cry of heresy fell upon Irving's astonished ears. He had been preaching upon the human nature of Christ and claiming that because He was human He must have been "tempted in all points like as we are." A man of the deepest sympathies himself, few have felt more keenly the full meaning of the words, "Himself bore our griefs and carried our sorrows," and "was in all points tempted like as we are," and to him in an unusual degree Christ was more pre-eminently human than any other man who has worn the veil of flesh, at the same time that he was also to him God enshrined in flesh. He had been speaking very freely of the brotherhood of Christ and His pity even for the tempted and fallen, not forgetting as he went on the Divine fellowship. A Mr. Cole among his hearers, a churchless clergyman with plenty of time for heresy-hunting, bred in the extremest school of the old theology, was horrified by the idea that temptation eould have had any power over Christ the sinless, and followed Irving into his vestry to ask if he really meant what he had been saying. Of course he replied that he did, quoting the Scriptures to sustain his position. Cole rushed away, inflamed with theological anger, and in a day or two burst into print with the most violent invectives against Irving's theology. Thus another train was laid, with occasional additions from Cole, of supplies for the coming disaster.

About this time Irving went as was his wont when seeking rest from city service, on a walking tour through Scotland, preaching often two or three times a day, spending hours in earnest conference with friends whom he visited

by the way, whose thoughts were like his own.
Wesley's great work among the English poor,
culminating in the powerful Methodist church,
had been crowned by his triumphant death just
before Irving's birth; but the work he had so
wondrously begun was still going on, while on
other theological lines Maurice, Newman and
Martineau, each still in his early manhood,
were unconsciously preparing for the work set
for them to do; and now, to Scotland, was coming a new wave of deepening and uplifting
spiritual life. Scattered at various points in
the land, among laymen such men as Erskine
of Linlathen, and in the pulpits Campbell of
Row and Story of Rosneath and many another
as devout yet now forgotten teacher, were
eagerly bending forward and listening as they
believed to calls to Christlier living and clearer
visions of the coming kingdom of God. Of
these, Campbell, although Chalmers said of
him later, "His was the most saintly soul I
have ever known," was to precede Irving to
the pillory;—he also was to be tried before his
own Presbytery, and judged, not by the testimony of his peers, but by casual hearers of
every rank and every degree of intelligence.
He also was to be silenced, yet his memory still
lingers among readers of old Christian literature like the fragrance of a broken box of
ointment. Erskine in his quiet study, a place

that proved safer than a pulpit, sent forth such works as "The Unconditional Freeness of the Gospel," and, judged by its author's peers in Christian thought and scholarship, the work made its mark on true thinkers, while the author, as a literary man, was safe from theological persecution.

It was inevitable that Irving's own spiritual consecration should have been deepened and enlarged by conferences with such men as these, and that with ever increasing earnestness he should have believed in the speedy coming of the kingdom of God, thus by a few years foreshadowing the coming to our day of such men as D. L. Moody of the world's ministry, Dr. A. J. Gordon of Boston, and hundreds of others of our most consecrated men.

On his vacation tours from and to London, crowds of working men were anxious to listen even on week-days, to Irving's preaching, and as they were only able to attend his services before five o'clock in the morning or after nine in the evening, he was accustomed to preach before five and after nine to large congregations gathered from the neighboring localities. In some of the cities crowds of from ten to twelve thousand gathered in the open air to hear him; and such was his control of his voice that the listeners on the outskirts heard him distinctly, while those near him were not

MAN, PREACHER, PROPHET 67

conscious of unpleasant effort. Certainly no common message from any common man could have attracted crowds at such untimely hours, or massed such audiences in the streets; and it is said that in the cottages where he rested, the poor listened as eagerly as did those of earlier days to his Master.

Returning invigorated to London, Irving pressed on with increased zeal in the multiplying labors that came to him. The annual conferences at Albury came and went and in them he entered into deep spiritual communion with men outside his own denomination, in whose minds he is said to have assisted in developing the thought of the Broad Church, since so important in the Church of England. The majority of the Alburians were Churchmen and by his intimate association with them, meeting and speaking with them, and now and then welcoming them into his own pulpit as if they were indeed his brethren in Christ Jesus, Irving was laying broad the foundation for one of the two charges that led to his deposition. One can never think of the great men then pressing forward in the Church of England, of that great Church's freedom in non-essentials, of the high service she was and is rendering and is to render to the world at large—one can never recall these things, while still remembering all that was steadily drawing nearer to

Irving, even to the breaking in sunder of his uncompleted years and the temporary thwarting of his message to the world, without a sense of inexpressible regret that that great sheltering and strengthening Church had not won him permanently into its communion; and yet in that case the world would have lost the lesson of one of the sublimest overcomings in its later years.

About this same time, too, one Alexander Scott, still a Probationer, but in those days a man of such rare clearness of thought and appreciation of spiritual truths that a great future which he failed to achieve was expected for him, came into Irving's friendship and helped to deepen, though he does not seem to have originated, the lines of thought in which Irving was treading. Irving was more and more looking forward to the coming of the kingdom of God, and in connection with the men before referred to—Campbell, Story and Erskine—in his books and by his sermons broadcast was awakening, especially in Scotland and in London, ever deepening interest in the reviving messages of the gospel. In many of the towns as well as in many of the humble cottages of Scotland, new heights and depths in God's inexhaustible love and power seemed awaiting the acceptance of saintly souls. Who can estimate the force of the marvelous sense of being permitted to touch by faith the divine love and power, that is able fully to redeem, able to give health of soul and health of body as well. And yet bodily healing had not thus far even entered into their imaginations, for these humble Christians were conscious only of deepening rest in God and a strange indescribable sense of His nearness to them.

We do not profess in any degree to be able to understand, much less to explain, the remarkable phenomena we are about to describe; but into this restful and prayerful atmosphere, unheralded, came events strangely like similar ones that occurred to the early Christians and, one would think, might have been received as indications of coming blessing, rather than of evil, by a devout church, and that yet were destined to become the cause of much heart-burning and to be smothered by conscientious though timid Christians before they were in any degree understood. The day of William James and his "Varieties of Religious Experience" had not then dawned, and disaster to existing conditions seemed imminent. There has been and still is so much misconception concerning what were called the "Gifts of Tongues," and "Healing," that we perforce give a somewhat detailed account of their origin in which, by the way, Irving had no part unless, as all Christians profess to believe, prayer is an active power with God. In London he and his people had certainly been praying for the return of the "Gifts."

The advent of "The Tongues," so-called, was on this wise: On a little farm near Fermicarry at the head of the Gairlock, not far distant from Glasgow, lived a family named Campbell, noted for its quiet simplicity and unusual saintliness. Their peculiar traits even in sorrowful circumstances, had awakened a deep sympathy in all, notably among their wealthier neighbors. A sister, Isabella, had died a while before, leaving such an impression of holiness that had she been a Catholic, her home would have become the shrine of the countryside. A younger sister, Mary, had inherited many of her sister's characteristics physically and spiritually. She too was apparently in the last stages of tuberculosis and supposed by all to be rapidly nearing the end. Thought by others to be dying, she like many another consumptive, seemed to cling strangely to life and to hopes of future usefulness. Irving, who was later attracted to the scene by what occurred there before his visit, may describe it: "It was on the Lord's day; and one of her sisters, along with a woman friend who had come to the house for that end, had been spending the whole day in humiliation and fasting and prayer before God with special respect to the restoration of the

'Gifts.' They had come up in the evening to the sick chamber of their sister who was laid on a sofa, and along with some others of the family were engaged in prayer. In the midst of their devotion the Holy Ghost came with mighty power upon the sick woman as she lay in her weakness, and constrained her to speak at great length and with superhuman strength in an unknown tongue, to the astonishment of all who heard, and to her own great edification and enjoyment in God, 'for he that speaketh with a tongue edifieth himself only.'" Thus, apparently without human agency, certainly without Irving's, came the gift of tongues, whose toleration was later to be one of the cogent reasons for condemning Irving as a half insane fanatic.

Just across the Clyde, in the little town of Port Glasgow, lived at the same time another family, as noted among their friends for religious sincerity and humility as were the Campbells among theirs. The fame of the Campbells was so widely spread that many had heard of their religious experiences who did not know them personally. The McDonalds were among this number. In this family were two brothers, ship-builders, plain, quiet Christian men, and an invalid sister. They too were soon to be singled out from their neighbors and to stand forward in a new and unlooked-for prominence in their little world. Familiar probably with the report of Isabella's character, it is supposed that they did not know of Mary's experiences, and we do not even know the name of their sister. It was the experience, not the person, that seems to have produced the profound impression this event created. One day, the brothers entering their home, found their sister in an agony which in their distress they supposed to be the pangs of death. Going to her bedside, "she at once addressed her brothers," as their own simple story tells, "at great length, concluding with a solemn prayer for James that he might *at that time* be endowed with the power of the Holy Ghost. Almost instantly James calmly said, 'I have it.' He walked to the window and stood silent for a minute or two. Those who saw him trembled, there was such a change upon his whole countenance. He then with a step and manner of the most indescribable majesty walked up to her bedside and addressed her in words from the twentieth Psalm— 'Arise and stand upright.' He repeated the words, took her by the hand, and she arose." From that time her health was perfectly restored and she went out and in among them as one endowed not only with a restored life but with new powers.

A few days later James wrote to Mary

Campbell, then supposed to be in the last stage of consumption, and addressed to her the same words he had spoken to his own sister. Conscious as yet only of the new gift of tongues, and realizing more clearly than at any previous time the exhausting power of her dread disease, she had given up all hope of continued life and was calmly facing death. James McDonald's letter was read to her. She lay still for a few moments and then in obedience to the call spoken by no audible voice, but, as she felt, dictated by the Holy Spirit, asked for her clothing, rose and dressed herself, and pale and emaciated still, and at first with feeble steps, but calmly ignoring her physical weakness, took her place again in the family circle. These experiences of the Campbells, already noted for their saintliness among all their acquaintances, made them of course one of the most conspicous private families in that part of Scotland. As a proof of Mary Campbell's entire restoration to health we may add that she later married, reared a large family and died aged, maintaining to the end her high saintly character. The McDonalds, however, always retiring, shrank from all publicity, maintaining to the end their godly simplicity of life. In these two families, strict Presbyterians, started more than eighty years ago a line of bodily healing without money and without price, that there seems every reason to believe should have continued and broadened in beneficent growth, had not the church turned its back upon the early teachings of its Master, and damming up the original stream, allowed it later to force its way through other channels, thus greatly undermining the church of to-day by substituting a modern for the Christ-given order of things, but proving by the glad acceptance of that imperfect substitution that the original truth is again to come duly into full acceptance, making the church what its Founder designed it to be—a refuge for the sick as well as for the sinful, and proving that even to-day the weakest and saddest may be re-born into entire newness of life.

About the same time in a different class of society, entirely removed from the influence either mental or spiritual of these humble folk, an educated lady, the daughter of a clergyman of the Church of England, accustomed to the quietness and well-ordered regularity of the more formal modes of worship in that communion, learned to her infinite blessedness that God's gifts sometimes far surpass man's expectations, and that in every communion God finds his own. We condense her own statement of the case, which, by the way, she prepared by her father's request. Attacked by hip disease, she went through a course of treatment

MAN, PREACHER, PROPHET 75

by skillful physicians, but returning home after this treatment found herself still unable to walk, making the attempt once or twice, but suffering much from her efforts. She was soon wholly confined to her couch. Eight years after the disease seized her, still almost a helpless invalid, one day in October, 1830, a friend called upon her who had known of her suffering and had been led to pray earnestly for her recovery. He asked in faith and God graciously answered his prayer. In her own words she says: "Rising to leave, Mr. G. put out his hand and said, 'It is melancholy to see a person so constantly confined.' I answered, 'It is sent in mercy.' 'Do you think so? Do you think the same mercy could restore you?' God gave me faith and I answered, 'Yes.' 'Do you believe Jesus could heal as in old times?' 'Yes.' 'Do you believe it is only unbelief that prevents it?' 'Yes.' 'Do you believe that Jesus could heal you at this very time?' 'Yes.' (Between these questions he was evidently engaged in prayer.) '*Then*,' he added, 'get up and walk to your family.' He then had hold of my hand. He prayed to God to glorify the name of Jesus. I rose from my couch quite strong. God took away all my pain and we walked down stairs. Dear Mr. G. prayed most fervently, 'Lord have mercy upon us. Christ have mercy upon us.'

Having been down a short time, finding my handkerchief left on the couch, taking the candle I fetched it. The next day I walked more than a quarter of a mile, and on Sunday from the Episcopal Jews' Chapel, a distance of one mile and a quarter. Up to this time God continues to strengthen me, and I am perfectly well; to Jesus be all the glory.

"It is material to add that my legs, the flesh of which was loose and flabby, feeling them in a short time after I walked down, were firm as those of a person in full health. The back, which was curved, is now perfectly straight. My collar-bones have been pronounced by a surgeon to be in quite a natural state, whereas one of them was before much enlarged.

"I must tell you that my mind had not been at all occupied with those events which had taken place in Scotland; indeed, all that I had heard concerning them was that a young person had been restored in answer to prayer; this was perhaps five or six months back. I had heard of nothing since, and can with truth say my mind had never been led to the contemplation of such subjects. I had not the least idea that my dear friend was offering up prayer in my behalf, for he did not say so until after the mighty work was wrought; he then said, 'This was my errand, for this I have been earnestly praying;' and with all humility gave the glory to Jesus, to whom be all might, majesty and dominion.

"Elizabeth Fancourt."

It has been claimed, and we believe without dispute, that each of these three cases was thoroughly authenticated, and the cures permanent. It is also, we believe, perfectly safe to claim that many corresponding cases—cases we mean of perfect cure through simple faith—have occurred both in Catholic and Protestant communions, and, to remove even the suspicion of hypnotism, or any mental collusion, often in cases where the sufferer, entirely unaided by the personal presence of any praying friend, was alone with God in prayer. Studying the manifestations carefully, one faces this question, difficult to answer: Had the Church of Christ eighty years ago cherished these gifts, instead of trying to stamp them out as evil, what standing room in the world would have been left for the confusing claims of the many varied forms of mental healing of to-day? But important and blessed as these unexpected experiences were to those who felt their healing power, this new development ushered in what has seemed to the world a most disastrous ending to Irving's course—disastrous or glorious as one measures it by natural standards or by Christly standards.

Slowly as news traveled in those days, Irving

at the center of religious thought must soon have heard of the remarkable experiences in these three distinct but equally consecrated families; and his heart already looking to God for the renewal of the early "Gifts," must have throbbed with inexpressible joy—a faith and joy which he freely shared with his own people, to the quickening of their prayers with his own for similar blessings. We may note in passing that in the first meeting at Albury in 1825, Irving probably received his first inspiration to hope for the renewed "Gifts" which he had supposed superseded when the immediate occasion for them passed, by the strong assertion of the Rev. J. Haldane Stewart, a noted clergyman of the Church of England, who mentioned the success he personally had had in promoting meetings for special prayer for the outpouring of the Holy Spirit and for the promise of "the latter rain," made in Joel. In the discussion that followed, another, supposed to be the Mr. Drummond earlier described, also a churchman, said:

"The miraculous gifts of the Spirit ceased not because they were no longer of use to the Church, but because the faith of the Church grew cold and dead. The Roman Church maintains that we Protestants have no ground whatever for saying that miracles were ever to cease, and that we can produce no warrant from Scriptures for saying so. In this she is right, and if the faith and purity of the Church burned as bright now as in the days of the Apostles, she would again exhibit that light to the world."

This, so far as we know, was the first expression of faith in our times, by a Protestant, in the supernatural gifts of the Spirit as the permanent endowment of the Church. To a soul like Edward Irving's, thirsting for truth whencesoever it came—from Jewish, Roman or Protestant lips,—these words from men whom he could fully trust, proved of mighty import, broadening his hope, deepening his consecration, and enlisting all his powers in the enlarged hopes he saw opening before the Church of God. A year or so later in a "Homily on Baptism," he used this expression, "In the grace of God under which the baptized are brought" (he was speaking for all the baptized, children as well as adults), "it is promised that they shall receive the gift of the Holy Ghost." As far as we can judge, the presence of the Holy Ghost had been neither expected nor desired unless in quiet guise in the ordinary churches of that day, and such expressions, as well as prayers for the renewal of the gifts, soon made Irving a still more marked man among his fellow ministers, and during the last years of his life led him through conflicts and sufferings which he met with a noble endurance that lends a tragic interest to his history. We can in no wise explain the coming or the ceasing of these deep spiritual experiences. We refer to them simply as necessary to indicate his position, and the reasons by which he vindicated his course.

If "in me ye shall have peace," was attesting itself as true, to him, "in the world ye shall have tribulation," was to prove itself no less true. The Church at large did not realize that the doctrine of the human nature of Christ as Irving presented it, might prove to be one of the most vital spiritual truths as yet revealed to man; that in the Incarnation might be the scientific answer to the greatest problem in natural law that man was to face; the Incarnation bridging the gulf between man as human and men uplifted by it into sons of God. It did not even dream that it stood facing new recallings of truths, which, accepted, would bring again into startling clearness a truth obscured for centuries, that in Christ men had been made sons of God, and through Christ had already entered into a new dispensation. This, Edward Irving was simply striving to make clearer to the comprehension of the Church; but the Church, bound in theological formalisms, forgetful of her supernatural baptism, turned upon Irving and his associates with what it believed to be holy horror toward men striving to destroy the Church of God. There is no doubt whatever that those arrayed against Irving believed themselves the actual conservators of Christian truth, and any one an enemy of the truth who disagreed with them.

CHAPTER IX

Other Ministers Charged with Heresy. Mr. Irving's Book, "Human Nature of Christ," Severely Handled. Advent of "Tongues" in his Church, July, 1831. Opinions of Carlyle and Others. Clear Statements by Henry Drummond and Rev. W. W. Andrews. Mr. Baxter's Defection. Modern Psychological Statement Concerning "Gift of Tongues."

In the meantime, lesser lights than Irving were being dealt with summarily by their Presbyteries. Among others, Campbell of Rowe, whom Chalmers had called "the holiest man I ever knew," had been deposed for teaching that all the world stood on common ground as regards the love of God, and all who would, might be saved. For this assertion alone, the Church of Scotland cast him out.

Fearless as was Irving, there could be little question of the fate that would sometime overtake him, and into it he must have walked with open eyes, for abundant fuel was soon to be added to his pyre. About this time in the London Presbytery, consisting of three members besides himself, after much irregular proceeding and the misquoting of his teachings, he was censured for his book on the human nature of

Christ, but as he had been ordained by a Scotch Presbytery, an English Presbytery could not depose him and he stood calmly upon his rights and went quietly on his way, upheld manfully and trusted as of old by his own church in Regent's Square. His book on the human nature of Christ was severely handled by the London Presbytery and severely criticised in the pulpits of that Presbytery.

To a generation that ranks Dr. Fairbairn as one of its theological standard bearers and calmly accepts his doctrine of the passibility of God,—that God can suffer in proportion to His being,—it must require little theological strain to think with Irving that Christ did have a human nature, that he could have sinned, that he must have suffered even unto blood striving against sin.

To allow Mr. Irving to speak for himself as to what he had really written on this subject we give somewhat copious extracts from the tract and from other deliverances on the same topic, for two reasons, first to show simply what he believed on the subject as distinguished from what he was reported as believing; also because we believe that thoughts so vital have a message for every generation, second only to the teachings of the Gospels. Wonderful as is Irving's style, the truths he declares glorify the style, as a pearl of great price does its setting.

"The point at issue," he says, "is simply this: whether Christ's flesh had the grace of sinlessness and incorruption, from its proper nature, or from the indwelling of the Holy Ghost:—I say the latter!"

"The precious truth for which we contend is, not whether Christ's flesh was holy—for surely the man who saith we deny this blasphemeth against the manifest truth—but whether during His life it was one with us in all its infirmities and liabilities to temptation, or whether, by the miraculous generation, it underwent a change so as to make it a different body from the rest of the brethren. They argue for an identity of origin merely; we argue for an identity of life also. They argue for an inherent holiness; we argue for a holiness maintained by the person of the Son, through the operation of the Holy Ghost. They say, that though His body was changed in the generation, He was still our fellow in all temptations and sympathies; we deny that it could be so; for change is change; and if His body was changed in the conception it was not in its life as ours is. In one word, we present believers with a real life; a suffering, mortal flesh; a real death and a real resurrection of this flesh of ours: they present the life, death, and resurrection of a changed flesh; and so create a chasm between Him and us which no knowledge, nor even imagination, can overleap.

And in so doing, they subvert all foundations: there is nothing left standing in our faith of Godhead, in our hopes of manhood."

ON THE TEMPTATION

"If His humanity bore not His human encounter, but needed the aid of His superior faculties, then how serveth it as an encouragement or an example to us who are mere men, and have no such divinity to bear us up? His humanity sustained Him against all earthly encounters; and whatever His divinity served Him, it served not to lighten the load which lay heavy upon His shoulders.

"I speak not now of the mere inward struggles which He had to maintain as the surety of mankind. Neither do I speak of those unrecorded temptations of the powers of darkness which He had to sustain throughout His life, and of which we have a shrewd intimation in the expression with which this recorded temptation concludes, 'The devil departed from Him for a season'; nor of the hidings of His Father's countenance, nor of anything save the outward visible sufferings with which men can sympathize. It may be said many of His followers have endured as much; but hath any one endured it without sin? To endure is nothing. The tortured Indian endures many crucifixions. Bed-rid patients endure whole years of torture, of which single nights have in them materials of many a tragedy. Nature must endure what the hand of God layeth on, however great it be. But doth she endure without murmuring, even what she cannot avoid enduring? And what is laid upon her by every wicked son of Belial, doth she endure without the resentment of a man? But here is a man, a very man, by distinction the Son of man, enduring heaps of trouble and affliction from every outward and inward quarter, and carrying Himself under it, not like a man, but like a God. This was the trial, not that He should bear, but that He should bear as one who bore not; not that He should endure in a sinful world, but that without sin He should endure; that for all His cruel condition He should be able to challenge the severest inspection of that host of enemies He was surrounded with, and who had risen up against Him; that He should bear the knowledge of Him who searcheth the heart and trieth the reins of the children of men, and received the testimony that He had done no violence, neither was any deceit in His mouth. Such was the heavy work which Christ undertook and such the happy issue to which He had to bring it.

"Having before Him this yet unattempted work of conquering in flesh and blood all the enemies of flesh and blood, both on earth and in hell, of preserving Himself immaculate though a man, perfect and sinless though a sorely tempted man, it was very desirable that He should have at the outset of such a perilous voyage some trial of His strength to endure its hardships. Having a human soul full of anticipation and feeling, as we see through all His life, especially in the garden of Gethsemane, He could not look upon the trial before Him without misgivings. If, after having proved His strength in this wilderness, and through all the scenes of His ministry, such horrors overtook Him on entering the last scene of it, what anxieties and fears must have pressed Him at its outset, when, from being a private man, He undertook so high a task! Think not I lower His dignity thus to behold Him accessible to those troubles of the spirit. It doth but prove the more the tenderness of His humanity, and encourage that fellow-feeling with Him which is the most genuine mark of His disciples. But take from your idea of His dignity or not, it is the truth that He had such misgivings, and prayed His Father in His agony to let the cup pass from Him. We have been so much agitated with disputes about His divinity that we dare hardly trust ourselves to conceive of His humanity, lest we should trespass upon the integrity of the former. But this nervous delicacy must not be indulged either by you or by me; we must look upon His true humanity,

and speak of it as the evangelists and the
apostles likewise spoke of it. And when need
is, we must do the same of His divinity. These
misgivings of the human soul of Christ, it was
the purpose of this temptation to chase away:
—to give Him, in the very outset and beginning
of His undertaking, a proof that He was equal
to its utmost perils; that He might take courage and enter upon it with boldness; that in
all His difficult passages memory might have
a spot to flee to, whereat He encountered this,
and more than this. This temptation I consider to be one of three remarkable passages
of the same kind, which are recorded in His life.
The other two are the transfiguration and the
agony."

. . . "This is the redemption, this is the
at-one-ment which was wrought in Christ, to redeem the will of a creature from the oppression
of sin and bring it to be at one with the will of
the Creator:—" *Preface to "Our Lord's
Human Nature."*

During these passing years, repeated bereavements had come to Irving and his wife in
the deaths of little children, but the union between them had grown steadily deeper and
stronger with each successive sorrow or trial
till they stood united in a perfect union that
nothing earthly was to mar or break. Albury

MAN, PREACHER, PROPHET 89

still influenced Irving greatly, seeming to give him in each visit renewed strength and inspiration. Passing once from Albury to Ireland for a week of rest for himself and his wife, in what would hardly seem rest to an ordinary man, he preached thirteen times in the week to audiences crowding churches to suffocation while crowds were seated outside the churches listening through the open windows. In all these services leading Catholics as well as Protestants were present, proving that not only in the Church of England was Irving arousing deep interest in his teachings but also among thoughtful Roman Catholics. It may, we think, safely be claimed that in his day through the universal hunger for truths that had lain silent, Irving's preaching met a general response from all classes and conditions of men, whatever their respective creeds. The truths he preached drew them far more than his magnificent personality, powerful as that was, and left them with a deepening hunger for truth.

After his return to Regent's Square supposedly rested, Irving turned to his people with power both simplified and intensified by his own deepening spiritual life. All the old power of his oratory remained. That was inevitable as part of himself; but he was more and more merging into quiet strength, and striving to help his people to turn wholly to God and in

Him find for themselves all the grace and power in His bestowal. The preaching services still went on as of old. But prayer and personal work by him and his people grew more and more dominant. Their daily six-thirty morning prayer-meetings drew large crowds of earnest Christians, and prayers for the gift of the Holy Spirit were constantly offered. Week by week tidings were received of the deepening work of the Spirit in Scotland and of the actual return of the gifts of the early Church, and there is no doubt that Irving and his people longed for similar manifestations of God's presence, which presently often appeared in their prayer-meetings.

For a time all was as orderly in their regular church services as of yore; but suddenly one Sabbath day in the midst of one of Irving's most solemn sermons, a woman previously distinguished for her great quietness and personal sanctity, rose from among the congregation and hastened into the vestry, closing the door behind her, but giving way while alone to one of the intense manifestations that had hitherto appeared only in their private services. This was the end of quiet services in the Regent's Square Church. Many such manifestations occurred later, and between "The Tongues," as they were called, during the attempts at worship by Irving and his congregation, and the crowds who hastened Sunday after Sunday to listen or jeer, as their tastes inclined them, there was henceforth no peace for Irving or his people. At all the services the church was so crowded that fears were entertained of a repetition of the Kirkcaldy disaster; and the London papers were full of witticisms and jibes at the expense of Irving and his people, and many of his intimate friends supposing him responsible for the uproar, believed that he was losing his reason and leading his flock into all manner of delusions. For the last time Carlyle and his wife listened to Irving in his pulpit. Carlyle describes the service characteristically and adds: "Poor Jean was on the verge of fainting and did not recover the whole night."

We confess that to us, Carlyle's description of the service and its effects seems a sad misunderstanding of the real character of his dearest friend while that friend was probing with all the loyalty that was in him, new and unexpected, and, to him not fully understood, conditions that he did not dare to suppress simply because, as he himself said later, during his trial before the Presbytery, he did not understand them and therefore could not tell whether they were, or were not, answers to the prayers of his people for the gift of the Spirit.

If one were forced to base his conclusions of the matter on the testimony of irresponsible newsmongers and the reports of captious critics one might indeed suppose that for a time Irving did lose his mental balance and that an epidemic of religious madness held high carnival in the Regent Square church. But providentially we have several calm, dispassionate descriptions of the occurrences at this very period. The writer of the longest of these descriptions was Mr. Henry Drummond, previously sketched in one of our earlier chapters, and thus strongly etched by Rev. W. W. Andrews:

"The late Mr. Henry Drummond, one of the keenest and most sarcastic intellects of the day, and a remorseless hater of shams and pretenses; as fearless in exposing, as he was sharp-sighted in detecting, all impostures and charlatanry; a man whose whole character was in antagonism to the fanaticism that is bred in excited crowds; of the highest culture, and the widest acquaintance with society; who had already been a member of Parliament, and sat again (long after Irving's death), from 1847 to his death,—twelve or thirteen years—as the representative of his county;—this man, who won for himself the universal respect of the country by his independence, his boldness, his integrity, and his sound conservative principles, which yet never carried him into factious opposition to any administration, not only believed in the reality of the spirtual manifestations, but was himself the subject of them. His own account of his experience is as follows:—

"'So soon as the manifestations occurred in London, I watched them narrowly; I found persons uninstructed in the schools of theology, pouring out a mass of doctrine, condensed into a few abrupt sentences, such as no living divine could utter. I heard everything they said tend to exalt Jesus and to abase the creature; I felt a sympathy in all that was expressed with something within myself; I experienced the spoken word to be like a two-edged sword, dividing soul and marrow, and discerning the thoughts and intents of the heart, in the detection and rebuke of sin. Although I soon found my requests answered by a greater spirit of grace of supplication being given me, and by a fuller realization of God as Love— and consequently a greater confidence in Him than I ever had before—nothing particular occurred until the 29th of the abovementioned July (1832), when, during an utterance of the Spirit through Mrs. Caird, which, however, contained nothing remarkable, either in word or manner, I felt an extraordinary anxiety for the souls of men, and particularly for some persons present, and a most earnest desire that they should enter into Jesus before the door was shut, upon His coming to judgment, which then appeared peculiarly near; so that I was constrained to cry out to all present, with a loud voice, to "enter now." This took place at family prayers in the evening; and as soon as they were over, I retired to my own room, and on my knees implored my Heavenly Father, if this were not excitement or delusion, to let it cause the same power to return quickly, and abide on me ever. Upon rejoining some other persons afterwards, I felt their most religious expressions cold to express the sensations I myself had; there was a realization of the presence of God in Christ, and of my own oneness with Jesus, diffusing a joy such as no words can describe; and just in proportion as I have been enabled ever since to abide all day long in Him, so is the power of the Spirit mighty within me to tell forth His mind and truth and praise. But I cannot command this power to come upon me; nor can I tell beforehand what will be given me to say, the subject and the power coming together; while, on the other hand, if I repress or withhold what I am prompted to utter, I feel a grief of the Spirit which must be experienced to be understood. I am therefore as conscious as I am of my existence, of a power within me, yet distinct from me; not using me as a mere machine, but bending my will and affections to love, to glorify Jesus; giving a peace and joy, and love to God and man, passing all understanding.' "

So much misunderstanding has always existed in regard to the "Gift of the Tongues," supposed by Irving and his people to be the manifestation of the baptism by the Holy Ghost, that we deem it right to give the statement of a man above criticism as to the actual events then occurring there. We refer to the Rev. W. W. Andrews, who furnished valuable data concerning this period. He was originally a Congregational minister for several years in Kent, Conn., where his memory is still fragrant among the older people. Becoming interested in the teaching of the Catholic Apostolic Church, he went abroad and made the intimate acquaintance of its leaders, later joining its fellowship and remaining a faithful and useful leader in the American branch of that church. He had planned to write a life of Edward Irving and had collected much material for it, which he generously allowed the writer to use as freely as she desired. Mr. Andrews died aged, some twenty years ago, near Hartford, Conn. We have selected Mr. Drummond's statement alone, from others, as strong, but written by unknown though educated men, and leaving this class of evidence epitomize Mr. Andrews' further statements as to the difficulties that surrounded Mr. Irving in his efforts to "try the spirits" now struggling for utterance. He acknowledges that among the uneducated and excitable members of the Regent Square Church, many abandoned themselves to mystical and unwarranted applications of scriptural passages, and supposed themselves inspired when in truth they were only excited, but as this was more than once true of people really devout, if ignorant, Mr. Irving strove to bring calm influences to bear upon them, while not hampering those who seemed like Mr. Drummond to speak simply and truly as the Spirit gave them utterance. Just at this time when London was loudly criticising the work among Mr. Irving's own people, a stranger appeared, who was to be a shining light among them for a few weeks, and then to change utterly his attitude, saying that he had been deluded and had deluded others. This man,—we use Mr. Andrews' information, but not his words,—an educated English lawyer, a devout churchman, had heard of the work in Mr. Irving's church, and came up to London to study the manifestations. Suddenly seized by the same influence,—the Holy Spirit as he then believed—he became at once one of the most active advocates of the new Gift. His education, his eloquence, and above all his apparent sincerity, made him at once a leader in the new movement. But as Mr. Andrews says, "without previous control from authority, and desir-

MAN, PREACHER, PROPHET 97

ing none," as soon as some prophecy of his did not materialize as soon as he expected, or as he had supposed it would, he at once said that he had been deceived or had spoken by a lying spirit. He at once withdrew from the Regent's Square church, and published a statement avowing his change of attitude. This startling defection only came to Mr. Irving's knowledge the evening before his final defense before the Presbytery after he had been told by them that he was not to be judged by the teachings of the Bible nor by the ancient creeds and standards of the Church of Scotland, but upon trivial violations of then accepted standards. His one reference to the defection of his "dear friend" is pertinent and we quote it: "Now no prophet since the world began has been able to interpret the time, place, manner and circumstances of his own utterances."

It only remains to add concerning Mr. Baxter that although he lived many years afterward, he could never decide whether he had been mistaken in claiming that he had spoken by divine inspiration or by some other. All he knew was that something outside himself possessed him in those days of strange experience. He lived and died, troubled by grave doubts as to the course he had pursued; of the pain, and to the extent of Mr. Baxter's ability, of the injury he inflicted upon the man who always spoke pityingly of him there could be no doubt.

Having given the Rev. W. W. Andrews' account of Henry Drummond's own statement and one other experience, one attributing the Gift of the Tongues to the Holy Spirit, and the other asserting that they came from a lying spirit, we think it only just to quote from a recent standard work—Dr. Cutten's "The Psychological Phenomena of Christianity"—in the chapter on Glossolalia—the Gift of Tongues.

Dr. Cutten states that experiences of this kind in Christendom are not confined to the primitive Christians nor to the early centuries of this era, but appeared in the thirteenth century among the Franciscans and still more recently during the last two centuries among the early Quakers and Methodists, and later still in the Catholic Apostolic Church, at one time improperly called Irvingites. Dr. Cutten asserts that upon the ignorant and superstitious these phenomena in others acted like wildfire, leading them into strange and bewildering excesses and to manifold contradictions.

Mr. Andrews says that just such excesses, mingled with the genuine manifestations in Mr. Irving's church, thus greatly increasing his labors and perplexities as he patiently tried to sift the tares from the wheat and prove what was from God and what was not.

If the question is asked why Mr. Irving himself did not share in the Gift of Tongues, one may add the further question, Why did not St. Paul speak of the first baptism of the Spirit at Pentecost, as did St. Luke, who was there and spoke of the things that he himself had seen and shared; while Paul, who was not present at Pentecost, always referred, when brought before his judges, to the vision he saw on the road to Damascus that turned him from a persecutor of the Nazarenes into one of their noblest supporters, and yet invariably spoke of the baptism of the Holy Ghost and the speaking of tongues as shared by him in common with most of the earlier Christians in much the same manner as did Mr. Drummond in his statement, Paul saying distinctly that he would rather speak five words in the common language than ten thousand in an unknown tongue because the five words would benefit his hearers and ten thousand bless only himself?

We may, we think, without reproof, assert that God knows better than man how to lift His individual servants into the highest communion with Himself. Luke may have found it at Pentecost; Paul on the road to Damascus, and Edward Irving in the everyday path of uplifting sorrow and whole-souled consecration to the Lord who became so real and so near to him as his days went on; while to many an uneducated man quietly but earnestly seeking after God has been given since Christ Himself appeared, wisdom and strength and power to receive and to follow even unto the death, if need be, God's deepest revelations of Truth.

CHAPTER X

Anxiety of Irving's Church Trustees. Irving Summoned before the London Presbytery. A Peculiar Trial. Remarkable Verdict. Deposed, May, 1832. Irving Enters Catholic Apostolic Church.

No one will question that a most serious problem presented itself to the trustees of the Regent's Square Church. Events were daily happening that Irving himself did not pretend to understand and that no person could control, and by all logic, even modern, the trustees of the church were forced to take action. It was a most painful position for every one. There were conferences with eminent lawyers and with Presbyteries, and finally Irving was cited to appear before the London Presbytery, already referred to as in serious doubts as to his orthodoxy, but able only to hear him, not to depose him.

For several weeks Irving and his people had foreseen coming disaster, but believing themselves following where God was leading, and amply able to defend their position by the teachings of the Old and the New Testaments, they went calmly on to meet the inevitable. Many of Irving's nearest friends did their best to persuade him to adapt his course to the customs of the Church, but while showing deep appreciation of their personal love, he was adamantine in his resolution to stand with his church on their rights to obey God as they understood Him.

Finally the trustees appealed to the Presbytery on the following points, summarized here, but still stated clearly:

First, that Mr. Irving has suffered and permitted and still allows persons neither ministers nor licentiates of the Church of Scotland to take part in the public services of the church.

Second, that he allows persons neither members of the church nor seat-holders, to do the same.

Third, that he allowed females to take part in the public services of the church.

Fourth, virtually the same as first.

Fifth, that he appointed times for the suspension of the usual order of worship for the exercise of the supposed "Gifts."

The first question really at issue was, Has the Holy Ghost manifested itself in the church at Regent's Square? If so, could any Christian Presbytery forbid its manifestations? A question not presented might have been, What would a Presbytery who forbade these manifestations have done on the day of Pentecost had they been in power? Doubtless every minister of the Presbytery had preached at various times on the story of Pentecost and prayed for the descent of the Holy Spirit, and it was, if not the bravest, at least the safest line to give to their examination in turning the question aside from the consideration of the Holy Spirit's presence and proceeding to try Mr. Irving on the acknowledged fact that he had allowed ministers and perhaps unordained members of other denominations, and still more, women, to speak in his church, and had changed somewhat the order of the service therein. Is there a Protestant church anywhere to-day that would consider such a course worthy of severe blame?

Irving had taken the ground from the beginning of the controversy that his course was fully justified by the teaching of the Bible and by the ancient standards of the Church, and expected to be justified by proving that he had fully followed this course. He seems to have had no doubt as to the result till to his amazement he was quietly told by the court that his course was to be judged without reference to the Bible but only to the trust deeds and the standards of the Church.

This statement once made and sustained by the court, nothing was left for Irving but to submit to whatever decision was made. He did this with dignity but with a solemnity and power that has had no parallel in later days. Believing as he did in the speedy coming of

Christ, and that although he could not explain them, the special experiences in his church had come as direct answers to his own prayers and those of his people, Irving stood before the Presbytery as St. Paul might have stood before Festus and Agrippa, pleading, not his own cause, but what he believed to be the cause of the Church of Christ.

His address was very long and may have seemed full of bombast to the impatient Presbytery listening to it. We give but the briefest summary. Referring to the exclusion of the Bible from the trial, and the substitution of the modern standards of the Church, he said pithily: "I entreat you to set up the Holy Scriptures as the only basis of faith and practice; to look as ministers, and to look as people to them alone; and I know this, that if you throw the Bible aside, you will not look to much else that is good. You may talk about standards as you please, but I know there will be little reading of the standards or other good books if there be not much reading of the Scripture. Therefore I entreat you to put the standards on their own basis, and every moment to walk before the Lord in His commandments. I tell you, O Presbytery, it will be a burdensome thing if ye do with a high hand and without examination or consideration, upon any grounds, upon any authority, shut up that house in which the voice

MAN, PREACHER, PROPHET 105

of the Holy Ghost is heard. Oh! if ye will turn aside from that and say, 'No, there are no customs or authority in the canons of the Church for it, and we will not consider whether the thing is in the Scripture or not; if ye will not consider it in the only true light—the light of the Scriptures—I tell you ye shall be withered in your churches, I tell you ye will be visited with heavy retribution; I tell you, the waters in your cisterns shall be dried up; I tell you, your flocks shall pine away for hunger and shall die. If ye will as members of a Christian court give your decision against me, while I deplore it on your account and that of the complainers, I rejoice, yea, I rejoice exceedingly for my own sake and the sake of my flock, that we are counted worthy to suffer shame and reproach for the testimony."

These words, spoken after two days of harassing trial and an intervening night of unceasing toil, by a man facing the utmost disgrace that the Presbytery could inflict upon him, yet believing in his own soul that he and his people were standing in the defense of the truth as it had been revealed to them, do not seem to the writer like the ravings of a madman but rather as the brave words of one like Paul facing his block or Peter standing beside his own cross. The words in which he foretold the disasters imminent to the Church of Scotland were often sadly recalled ten years later when the disruption of the Church took place through some of the very evils Irving had deprecated, and more than four hundred of its leading ministers, Chalmers at their head, were literally turned out with their people, from their churches and their manses, "without pastures or fields to feed their flocks"; and in the words of one of their leaders, "more than one thought sadly of Irving and their treatment of him, and wished that he were again among them."

There were one or two postponed meetings for what one must believe was from the beginning a foregone conclusion, and then after a most informal evening meeting the verdict was announced.

Before we quote the verdict given at the close of this strange trial, it will be well to state a few of the facts connected with the first so-called trial, for heresy in London a short time previously. It had been found illegal to pass any judgment upon Mr. Irving by any Presbytery save by the one in Scotland where he had been ordained. In addition to the fact that the London Presbytery had no jurisdiction over him, Mr. Irving had strenuously appealed against their unjust treatment of him in refusing to consider with him personally any errors they might find in his tract on the "Human Nature of Christ," and their misrepresentations of his printed statements, so that the first London investigation neither had any authority over him, even if he were proved heretical, nor had acted in accord with the ordinary methods of Presbyteries. This being true, the second Presbytery could have had no warrant for quoting the illegal verdict of the first. Probably, however, not caring to send down to Scotland for deposition, one of their most popular and useful clergymen on charges so trivial as those upon which he had been tried before them, they proceeded to bring in the following peculiar verdict—a verdict that does not in the remotest degree allude to the subject stated in his indictment or at his trial. This verdict, though stripped of its verbiage, is in substance strictly correct. We add only the fact that this verdict and the trial that preceded it were severely criticised by all the leading lawyers in the country, and it was said it could not have been rendered in any ordinary court of justice. We give the joint verdicts without further comment. "Whereas the said Rev. Edward Irving, having previously been delated and convicted before this Presbytery on the ground of teaching heresy concerning the human nature of our Lord Jesus Christ, has been declared to be no longer a member thereof, yet in respect that the trust deed of the said church legally drawn and concluded with the consent of the said Rev. Edward Irving, and the said trustees as parties thereto, expressly provides that this Presbytery shall or may act and adjudicate in all cases of complaint brought . . . against the minister of the said church . . . and the Presbytery . . . do find that the charges in said complaint are fully proven; and therefore do decern that the said Edward Irving has rendered himself unfit to remain the minister of the National Scotch Church aforesaid, and ought to be removed therefrom, in pursuance of the conditions of the trust deeds of the said church."

The Presbytery added that Irving must return to the church at Annan where he had been ordained and there be formally deposed in conformity with the rule of the Church making deposition possible only in the church of one's ordination. Annan, as we have said, was Irving's birthplace; in that same old church he had been baptized, later received into the communion of the Church; he had often gone joyously back and forth to the old town he loved so well; there, too, he had been ordained; and he once more was to go thither among his kinsfolk and old friends, branded as a heretic, to be deposed from the ministry, then to leave Annan forever,—its noblest, bravest, truest son.

The Sunday after the conclusion of his trial, for which Irving had foreseen no such ending, was to have been a more than ordinarily important one to him and to his people. Two hundred new communicants were to be received into the church, and not knowing whether the services of that day would or would not be interfered with, but hoping against hope, a large number had assembled for the six o'clock morning prayer meeting; they found the church doors locked against them and a notice that it was not to be opened again till other arrangements had been made. The people stood for a while dismayed in the street and then adjourned to a large hall in the neighborhood that happened just then to be vacant. During the week Irving went down to Annan as the Presbytery had commanded and the church was crowded to witness the exercises of his expulsion by the local Presbytery. For some reason the services were prolonged till late in the afternoon, when it became so dark that a candle had to be brought to the pulpit to render whatever reading was needed possible. It was a strange, sad scene—the congregation almost hidden from sight in the darkness, and the mental gloom deeper than the outward, resting heavily upon the people. Suddenly the Rev. David Dow, the Presbyterian minister of Irongray and therefore not a member of Irving's church, but a man who had often attended the Regent's Square services and believed that he had received the gift of the "Tongues," rose from his seat in the darkness and started towards the door, exclaiming as he went, "Arise, depart! Flee ye out! Ye cannot pray! How can ye pray to Christ whom ye deny? Ye cannot pray. Depart, depart!" After a moment Irving arose from his seat and followed him, not without protest from some of those present, but probably accompanied or followed by several of his other clerical friends who had come down with him from London to attend the trial. Of course the trial was never concluded; but to all intents and purposes, Irving was thenceforth an outcast from the Presbyterian church. He had made a most solemn appeal against the Presbytery, affirming what he really believed and not what men who did not know reported him as believing, but had been told by the Moderator that he seemed to think himself preaching to a London congregation, and not on his defense before the Presbytery.

Returning to London, Irving and many of his flock eventually allied themselves with the Catholic Apostolic Church, already established and flourishing, but he went among his new brethren simply as an ordinary member of the church; probably if he had lived he would have risen to eminence in that church, but his days were numbered. He said of himself one day sadly, "The reproaches of my brethren have broken

MAN, PREACHER, PROPHET 111

my heart"; but he tried bravely and patiently to adapt himself to the new rôle given to him. It seemed to some, Mrs. Oliphant among them, that the lowly place he occupied in his new church relations should not have been given to a man of his character and abilities; but Irving himself accepted the change in peace and quietness.

That there were issues imminent infinitely more serious than the placing of any man in a subordinate position, or even than the breaking of a noble Christian heart, has long seemed incontrovertible to some earnest thinkers. Tremendous changes that have not even yet reached their limitations stood immediately confronting not only the church at large but also the whole world.

Henceforth these two—Edward Irving on one side, the Presbytery on the other—went their parted ways: Irving soon to prove beyond a question that he had truly won the welcome: "Well done, good and faithful servant, enter thou into the joy of thy Lord"; this most cautious Presbytery to leave for Time to prove that by silencing the voice of one crying "Prepare ye the way of the Lord" and for awhile checking the stream of widening primitive Christian faith they had unconsciously earned the solemn condemnation of their Master, speaking to all the centuries and potent in their day as in ours, "In vain they do worship me, teaching for doctrines the commandments of men." They had debarred the Bible and deliberately preferred the Trust Deeds of their Trustees and the stated polity of their church; warranted, perhaps, by these it was easy by the vote of one small Presbytery, and that one not composed of the intellectual or spiritual leaders of their church, to send forth Edward Irving branded as a heretic.

They felt no foreshadowing of the problems even then imminent before all churches and the world at large, nor how soon the one sure refuge left to the church would be not its "Standards," but the full acceptance of the gospel in all its primitive purity, or its destruction from critical unbelief and the ignoring of Christly standards of love and faith. Who, today, can say what access of peace and indestructible faith might have been won to the churches as a whole had the work begun in those years in widely-varying communions been fostered to "see whereunto it would grow," instead of being sedulously trained to suit prudent modern standards? We know what the years have brought and where the world stands today, but we can only wonder where it might have stood had Christians cared less for "traditions of men and more for the clear teachings of Jesus Christ."

CHAPTER XI

Failing Health. Last Call on the Carlyles. Leaves London for Rest. Last Journey. Last Letter. "Dies unto God." Universal Mourning.

One more sore sorrow came to him in those days, and his youngest child faded slowly away, as Irving believed, from the land of shadows into the world of perfect communion and unhindered service, whither his father was so soon to follow him. It was evident to all who saw his prematurely aged and bent frame that Irving's strength and life were ebbing and he was finally persuaded by his anxious friends to go on one more journey in search of rest and strength. He still held strongly to the belief in God's power to give perfect health when needed by his children and he could not believe that his own work on earth was nearly ended, and he set forth on a horseback journey, planning to go through Wales to Scotland.

Carlyle shall describe to us his own and his wife's last glimpse of Irving:

"Edward Irving rode to the door one evening, came in and staid with us some twenty minutes—the one call we ever had of him here;" (in their latest London home, Cheyne Road;) "his farewell before setting out to ride toward Glasgow, as the doctors, helpless otherwise, had ordered. He was very friendly, calm and affectionate; chivalrously courteous to *her*, as I remember. 'Ah, yes!' looking round the room, 'you are like another Eve, you make every place you live in beautiful.' He was not sad in manner, but was at heart, as you could notice, serious, even solemn." Thus the three whose lives had been so notably united and divided, parted; Irving leaving them doubtless as he left all to whom he said farewell, with a solemn, tender benediction that held in it all he could possibly desire for any whom he loved, and thenceforth steadily faring down through the narrow gates of death up to the eternal and perfect service; the Carlyles going forward toward the more than thirty years of prosperity and growing fame that were to be theirs together, and afterward, to the world knows what, of underserved criticism and later, of justice.

Irving passing away from the pain and distress of his last months in London went slowly onward down through the "beautiful, solemn mountains of Wales," towards his Scottish destination. On the way he wrote many tender and hopeful letters to his wife and children, yet one sees, reading between the lines, that the writer is not growing stronger in bodily health.

Finally, caught in a severe shower, he rides on in extreme weakness to a "motherly inn" where he was "greatly tempted" to take the surgeon's advice. He says, "My spirits sank for one-half hour and I had formed the serious resolution of turning into the sick-room. But I remembered the words of the Lord upon my journey and ordered my horse and rode with great speed forward." This for a time seemed to relieve him. Stopping that night at another wayside house, still in great weakness, but declining medical aid, he drank copiously of hot tea and gruel and retired, finding, as he says, when he awoke that "God had so blest this treatment that at first I exclaimed, 'Can it be that I am entirely healed?' But I soon found that the Lord's hand is still upon me. Yet I am sure that I received a very great deliverance that night. To-day my headache has returned, with sickness."

In his letter of the next day he says: "Now, my dear, I write you again to express my decided judgment that you should not any longer be separated from me. My God is sufficient for me, I know, and He hath been my sufficiency during these three days and nights of the sharpest fiery trial both of flesh and heart which I have ever proved. . . . In the night seasons the Psalms have been my consolations against the faintings of flesh and heart."

On the day following he writes from Liverpool his last letter, saying to his wife: "At the same time, in your coming, if you see it your duty to come, proceed tenderly and carefully in respect to yourself, coming by such stages as you can bear. I hope you will find me greatly better under this quiet and hospitable roof. Be of good courage, my dear wife, and bear thy trials, as thou hast ever done, with yet more and more patience and fortitude. It will be well with the just man at the last. Now farewell. The blessing of God be upon you all.

Your faithful and loving husband,

EDWARD IRVING."

Leaving her three children, one of them a baby, at the earliest possible moment, his wife reached him, finding him greatly weakened in body but still indomitable in faith. After a few days, rested, and strengthened somewhat by her gentle ministrations, they started for Glasgow, the final stage in his journey. Not as he had come in his prime, full of the zest of consecrated hope; not to the activities of Christly living; yet stronger and braver in soul, despite his dying body, and to attain greater heights than he had ever before ascended, came Edward Irving and his suffering wife. There they were received with the tenderest welcome by their friends, the Taylors; and at their hospitable door Irving's earthly journeys ended. There were a few weeks of increasing weakness, yet of unfailing faith. He could not realize that his earthly days were drawing to a close. Once or twice before, his life had seemed miraculously prolonged, and full of faith and strong desire to serve God for many more years upon the earth, he still fully expected to be restored to health and active service. But his friends saw clearly that the end was rapidly approaching. Mrs. Irving's father and mother, Dr. and Mrs. Martin, and Mr. Irving's mother, joined Mrs. Irving in the care of her husband, while those at a distance who had known and loved him carried him in their sympathetic prayers. He seemed to have no anxieties for his own future nor for that of his family. A day or two before his death, his mother, then an aged woman, asked him who would care for his family if he should be taken away. "The elders of the church will care for them, mother," was his reply. He knew that in the Catholic Apostolic Church no member ever lacked any help or comfort that was needed, and that through that church, if in no other way, God would care for his family, as the future abundantly proved.

Then there came a Sunday morning, December 7, 1834, when, withdrawn from further conference with earthly friends, he entered upon his last conflict—alone with God. He was fording depths of physical pain and could no longer respond to the dear home voices, but amid the pangs of his fainting body, his soul still rested upon God. Hour after hour passed in the long, sore struggle. Over and over he repeated to himself strange, deep whispered words that none about him could understand, till Dr. Martin, bending over him, caught the words of the twenty-third psalm in Hebrew; then a little later came his last perfected sentence,—"If I die, I die unto the Lord," and thus he fell asleep, dying as he had lived, "unto the Lord," forgetting not when heart and flesh were failing him, and the shadows of the valley of death were pressing heavily, the central thought of his life—the Lord his God.

"Write, saith the Spirit, Blessed are the dead who die in the Lord, for they rest from their labors and their works do follow them." They laid him down to rest where his conflict had ended, and the most splendid of the Scottish churches, the Glasgow Cathedral, opened its doors to receive him and he was buried within its crypt. Thither to his burial, forgetting all that had seemed to them in their rigidity his mistaken faith, and remembering only his saintly life, his Christ-like brotherhood and his all-embracing sympathy, came from various parts of Scotland and from England, not only those who had stood shoulder to shoulder with him to the end, but those who had supposed themselves permanently estranged. It was a strange, sad, pitiful burial; for strong men do not weep easily, and many were there that day who could never thenceforth speak of him without tremors in their voices and pain in their hearts.

One can but wonder to how many of them came the sad prescience of the clouds that were soon to gather about their beloved church, rending it in twain, and literally fulfilling his prophecy as to hastening disasters. Still less was it possible for them to foresee the impending changes soon to envelop all Christendom. Not a man there was to live more than a quarter of a century longer without seeing with dismay the scientific and intellectual change that was to enshroud Christendom. Had Irving lived to the full measure of his days, he too would have had to face the changes that were coming; but no one who truly understood the man could for an instant doubt that whatever shreds of broken creeds, manmade, were to be rent away, nothing that could have come within the range of his powerful intellect could have caused him for an instant to cease to believe in God, the Creator and Father, in Christ the incarnate son of God and in the Holy Spirit the Eternal comforter. But they knew not what was coming and they left him to his rest in silence and peace. But if it is true that he rested from his labors, it is quite as true that his works have followed him.

The memory of God is a long, long memory, and no man can do an abiding work in His name and be forgotten by Him. Irving indeed rested from his labors and the world went its way; but he had taught strenuously certain truths half-forgotten in the many generations since the Master had first uttered them, and the truths obscured for a while by the deposition and disgrace of their teacher could not be buried in any crypt; and even though turned aside for a while and in the later guise less spiritual than as he presented them, have shaken many a church to its center in our own day.

Irving taught in all its fullness the Fatherhood of God, the brotherhood of Christ, the presence and power of the Holy Spirit, the power of faith to heal the sick and to cleanse the sinful. He believed in, too, and taught, the speedy coming of the kingdom of God. To many there was never a time when that kingdom seemed more remote and uncertain than it does to-day. But the kingdom of God cometh not with observation. Many a change has come to the material world since 1834, and to some it seems that even greater changes have come into Christendom, and that many an old-time creed is being swept from the face of the earth. But only a few knew for more than one generation that the faith of Christ had superseded the power of the Cæsars, and Paul and Huss and Savonarola and Latimer and Ridley and many another man and woman, saints of God, have laid down their lives defeated, as men spell Defeat, but victors as God spells Victor; and no man in his generation did more to foreshow the coming of the kingdom of God than did Edward Irving.

To-day, even so many years after his death, none of us may know, none foretell, what lies immediately awaiting the Church and the world. Yet we believe that the truths of science, sometimes so unjustly feared, when once fully understood, will establish forever the existence of a creative mind behind the laws through which He has worked through the long millenniums. Prophecy fulfilled, surprises as greatly those who live in the days of its fulfillment as it may have perplexed those who proclaimed it and looked forward to its fulfillment.

The divinest truths often seem incongruously

small in their beginnings. The stable at Bethlehem and the cross at Calvary promised little as the beginnings of a "kingdom that should have no end," and the Church of to-day, clasping in one hand shreds of crumbling creeds, and reaching forth the other for truths it can as yet neither fully understand nor interpret, is, we believe, standing in the dawn of a day to be great with the glorious revealings of God dwelling among men. We do not clearly know, we do not need to know what the immediate future is rapidly bringing to the world. Like Edward Irving we need only to know that while we live on the earth, whether in darkness or in light, "we live unto God," and that when we die, understanding God's perfect will or not, we "die unto Him."

CHAPTER XII

APPRECIATIONS

By

S. T. COLERIDGE.
THOMAS CARLYLE.
FREDERICK D. MAURICE.
EXTRACT FROM PERSONAL LETTER.
REV. JAMES HAMILTON, D.D.
REV. W. W. ANDREWS.
REV. GEO. LEON WALKER, D.D.
BARRY CORNWALL.
CHRISTIAN REMEMBRANCER.
FRASER'S MAGAZINE, JANUARY, 1835.
NORTH BRITISH REVIEW, VOL. XXXIX.
  (Attributed to Dr. Hanna.)
LONDON QUARTERLY REVIEW, VOL. XIX.
MACMILLAN'S MAGAZINE, VOL. VI.
  (Attributed to Rev. Robert Story.)

Presenting only a condensation of a large amount of material in the hands of the author for a life of Edward Irving, she deems it only just to her readers to give them in these Appreciations literal extracts from several articles published soon after his death by men who had known him well, and worked with him on lines of Christian service. Two of these articles were, however, written in later years by Americans—one by the Rev. Mr. Andrews, earlier described, the other by the Rev. Dr. George Leon Walker, a prominent Congregational clergyman, than whom during all his ministry no one more fully illustrated the same high consecration and remarkable spiritual power that controlled the man whom he so ably described in his article. The author feels that these extracts more than emphasize her own high estimate of Edward Irving.

"But I hold withal, and not the less firmly for these discrepancies in our moods and judgments, that Edward Irving possesses more of the spirit and purpose of the first Reformers, that he has more of the head and heart, the life, the unction, and the genial power of Martin Luther, than any man now alive; yea, than any man of this and the last century. I see in Edward Irving, a minister of Christ, after the order of Paul; and if the points, in which I think him erroneous, or excessive and out of bounds, have been at any time a subject of serious regret with me, this regret has arisen principally or altogether from the apprehension of their narrowing the sphere of his influence, from the too great probability that they may furnish occasion or pretext for withholding or withdrawing many from those momentous truths, which the age especially needs, and for the enforcement of which he hath been so highly and especially gifted."

S. T. Coleridge.

"His was the freest, brotherliest, bravest human soul mine ever came in contact with. I call him, on the whole, the best man I have ever (after hard trial enough) found in this world or now hope to find.

"Think (if thou be one of a thousand, and worthy to do it) that here once more was a genuine man sent into this our *un*genuine phantasmagory of a world, which would go to ruin without such; that here once more, under thy own eyes, in this last decade, was enacted the old Tragedy (and has had its fifth act now) of 'The Messenger of Truth in the Age of Shams.' . . .

"This man was appointed a Christian Priest; and strove with the whole force that was in him to *be* it. . . ."

THOMAS CARLYLE: Eulogy.

" I HAD no personal intercourse with the late Mr. Irving, and I heard him preach but rarely. . . . But I learnt lessons from some of Mr. Irving's books, which I hope I shall never forget. I recollect with gratitude portions of his sermons on the Incarnation of our Lord:—by some portions of them I was grieved. . . . What he taught me was to reverence the education he had received in the John Knox School, and the fathers who had imparted it to him. I had not that reverence before; I had shrunk from what I believed to be hard, narrow, and inhuman. He showed me that the old patriarchs of Scotland had a belief in God, as a Living Being, as the Ruler of the earth, as the Standard of Righteousness, as the Orderer of man's acts in all the common relations of life, which was the most precious of all possessions to them, the want of which is the cause of all feebleness and immorality in our age. He made me perceive how entirely different their godliness was from the sentimental religion, which consists in feelings about God; or from the systematic religion, which consists of notions about Him. He led me to see that unless we begin from God—unless we start from the conviction, that the thing which is done upon earth He doeth it Himself—the belief in Christ will pass into a belief in the mere Savior for us,—the belief in a Spirit will be at first a mere recognition of certain influences acting upon us, and will evaporate at last into pantheism.

"I perceived, clearly, that Mr. Irving had not acquired these convictions in England. He acknowledged—brave man as he was—his obligations to Coleridge as a teacher, at a time when such an acknowledgment was perilous, almost fatal, to his reputation with the circle which then paid homage to the young Scotch preacher. It now requires no courage for any man . . . to express the utmost depth of gratitude to that benefactor; still I am sure that what Irving owed to him, though it was theological lore in the strictest sense, was not this theocratic faith. That he brought with him; it was part of his convenanting, Calvinistical culture. As such I paid it, and still pay it, the profoundest homage. I have learnt since to honor the teaching of the English Church. I have to bless God for teaching which belongs to what calls itself the Catholic Church. But I have found nothing in either to supersede this. I have found nothing in either which is good without this. I reverence it as Protestant theology in the highest, purest meaning of that word, and as the very ground of all theology. . . .

"I thank Mr. Irving for showing me that if Protestantism is only a religious machinery, it must be a very bad religious machinery; that if it assumes its higher, diviner right, it will be stronger than ever it was—just because it cannot stand alone, but will demand a humanity as wide as its theology, and grounded upon that."

FREDERICK DENISON MAURICE.
From Introduction to "Doctrine of Sacrifice."

"SOON after this I went to B., and there continued in the work of the ministry during the remainder of Mr. Irving's life. I was not a member of his church, had never partaken of the Lord's Supper under his ministry, and had no partiality for Presbyterianism. B.

was then a long day's journey from London, where I had no business, but as often as I could, I took the journey, solely to attend his ministry, which I found the more instructive and valuable the more I heard it, and to cultivate his acquaintance more closely. From his instruction I learned more of Christian truth, and from his example more of the Christian life, than from any other man. I ever found his house a home to me, or if it should be already full, as it often was, then that of some of his friends, during very frequent visits to London.

"To a very large number of young men, earnest in purpose to devote themselves to God's service, and from various ranks of society, I found him to be, as to myself, a guide, a counselor, and friend, and his early, and I may call it, tragical death, left among us a blank which never can be supplied on earth again."

Extract from a personal letter to Rev. W. W. Andrews, written by one who, when he met Mr. Irving, was a young clergyman in the Church of England.

"FEW have, in these last times, more marvelously united the pastor and the prophet; consecrated genius and assiduous affection; that intellectual sublimity, which ennobles the topics which it touched, and that exuberant benignity which propitiated, and carries captive the objects of its continued forthflowing than did Edward Irving. His mind was like his heart, of the largest human size; and as he loved without effort, so he was inevitably eloquent. And because he squandered his brave thoughts and burning words on the most ordinary occasions, and in the midst of the littlest men, so the very consistency of his grandeur abated much of its effect, in a world which keeps its grandeur for set times and gala days. There was nothing vulgar in his make, and consequently nothing looked trivial in his eye. His mental furniture was all in keeping,—massive, unique, ample; and his vocabulary was the expression of his mind. Through the stained window of his rich-coloring fancy every landscape wore its luxurious gayety or its purple gloom; and in the silver basket of his idealism, the most common gourds shone through, like golden apples. And it was not his fault, but the world's, that life is not the thing of wonder, and nobility, and delight, which his creative eye beheld it. Hence came what is vulgarly called his vanity. No sort of vanity is good; but the most innocent is that which comes, as his did, not from the contempt of others, but from loving them too much. He only loved the praise of men so far as he loved themselves, and believed them sincere. It was men's hearts of which he was so greedy. Their huzzas and clapping hands he never hungered after. "Seldom have bigger thoughts and loftier sentiments struggled for expression in mortal speech, than those which are embodied in his magnificent 'Orations'; and though his practical wisdom did not keep pace with his discursive prowess, the might of his genius, and the grandeur of his views, and the prevailing solemnity of his spirit, gave a temporary lift to an earthly age. His presence was like Elijah's in the land of Israel, a protest against prevailing sins; and, like every protest in Jehovah's name, it carried a sanction and diffused an awe. And here lay his moral greatness. Here was the thing which truly made him a Hero. In each controversy he took what he believed to be the Lord's side; and in every audience spoke clearly out what he believed to be God's truth. With all his love of human love, he had no fear of man; even as with all his faithfulness, there mingled no atom of malignity. In the pulpit, as bold as the Baptist, he was in private a very Barnabas—a son of consolation. In his voice, and looks, and movements, such continual comfort—in his spontaneous sympathy, and exuberant joy, that perpetual cordial, which—an image of a better Friend—made no day dull on which he shone, and no dwelling desolate which still expected his visit. And whilst the multitudes came out to hear the prophet, the memories in which he now chiefly lives are theirs who knew him as the pastor. . . . "

Dr. James Hamilton.

From a sermon preached on an anniversary of the dedication of the Church in Regent's Square, by Rev. Dr. James Hamilton. Dr. Hamilton was Mr. Irving's successor in the Church in Regent's Square, and in the pulpit from which he had been deposed, and a religious writer of note.

"A STANCH Protestant and Presbyterian, he yearned after what was good and true in every communion, and had words of loftiest eulogy for the precious things and holy men of Rome; full of reverence for the treasures he recovered for the profit of his own times, he reached forward with joyful hope to the coming and Kingdom of his Lord; strong in his love, and bold in his assertion of personal freedom, he upheld with his whole heart the principle of obedience to authority. These oppositions of truth and counter-currents of feelings he could not perfectly reconcile, and this made him an enigma to his generation. There is no spirit of partisanship in him.

"He sought for the whole truth, and gave it forth as he learned it, without fear or partiality; and narrow men who clung to their parties and their shibboleths, were vexed and irritated. They saw a man whom no formulas

MAN, PREACHER, PROPHET 133

of theirs could measure, wild in his look, and terrible in his power, breaking their idols in pieces, and making the land to ring with the battle-cry of the coming King; and they knew that God was preparing to lead up His Church out of the dark night of the past into the glory of His kingdom, and that this man's work was to startle the sleepers and summon them to arise and gird themselves for the march.

. . . .

"He united in himself, without being able perfectly to reconcile them, the most varied religious elements. He was a Protestant in his strong individuality (the personal being as strongly developed in him as in Martin Luther); in his abhorrence of Romish superstitions and errors and tyranny; in his appreciation of the fullness of the Gospel, and of the power of the Cross of Christ; and in his strong assertion of the Will of the Father, and of His eternal, all-embracing purpose in His Son. He had recovered, also, the great truth of Patristic Theology, the Incarnation, the basis of all sound Christian doctrine, which the Reformers, and their successors still more, had too much lost sight of in contending for one of its fruits, the Atonement. And in addition to the noblest features of the Reformation, and of the age of the Fathers, he was holding up with great power the hope of the primitive Church, the return of the Lord Jesus Christ in the glory of the resurrection to rule the earth in righteousness.

"Mr. Irving died too soon to see whereunto the work would grow for which he had thus periled all things, and how signally the providence of God was to accomplish his vindication. Within ten years after his death, the Church of Scotland, of which he had said, 'That the General Assembly, Synods, Presbyteries, and Kirk Sessions, with all the other furniture of the church, are about, like the veil of the temple, to be rent in twain, or to be left like the withered fig tree, fruitless and barren, I firmly believe,' was after one of the fiercest struggles through which any Church ever passed, rent in twain. . . . The flock which followed him into exile, and were left without a shelter in the streets of London, now celebrates Divine service with majestic rites in a building worthy almost, for size and grandeur, to be ranked with the Cathedrals of England."

REV. W. W. ANDREWS.

"IF there has been in modern times a man with the old apostolic fire and fervor for the salvation of men and the glory of the Savior, Irving was that man. Into whatever mistakes as to the time of the millennial era or of the tokens of its coming he was led, it is impos-

MAN, PREACHER, PROPHET 135

sible not to see that human souls were dear to him and the honor of the Master above all. This is as manifest in the lowliness as in the splendor of his work. It shines out quite as conspicuously in his house-to-house visitations of the poor and wretched as in his majestic pulpit utterances and marvelous prayers, which fascinated and awed the crowds of wearied London worshipers. He loved men. He followed and sought them out as lost sheep. He sought the house of God and the honor of One who was humiliated and crucified for men.

"A saint of God was Edward Irving, and the Scottish Church, which censured and deposed him, can show few more brilliant or more sacred names than his, whatever his errors of judgment or mistakes of biblical interpretation. The church where first he preached in stated care of souls did well to open its doors to the deposed minister for funeral and for sepulcher. Long will it be before it can offer like sacred office to one whose name will enkindle recollections more noble and more tender."

REV GEORGE LEON WALKER, D. D.

Quoted from *The Independent*. Dr. Walker was pastor of the First Church, Hartford.

AT a meeting of a literary club which Irving had been expected to address, held soon after his death, Barry Cornwall (B. W. Proctor) read a paper from which we take the following extracts:

"Those who have been in collusion or coöperation with him that is gone alone can furnish facts sufficiently accurate and minute to form a true estimate of his character.

. . . .

"And more especially when it happens that through the importance of the services on the one hand, or the heat of contention on the other, a great man has been either too highly or too lightly esteemed by his contemporaries, it becomes the duty of all who knew him to state fully all they knew.

. . . .

"But our present purpose is not to eulogize; we merely wish to record a few instructive particulars concerning Edward Irving as a man and as a theologian,—in either of which characters he is justly appreciated by those only who have known him intimately and long. And in both these aspects, to those who knew him well, there was a progressive and accelerating advance towards perfection as he drew near the end of his course, the last years of his life being the most instructive, the most lovely as a man, the most exemplary as a Christian. . . .

"The first great feature in Edward Irving's character was godliness, and its correspondent deportment towards man, a reverence for station and authority. It was manifested in everything he did, in every word he spoke, that in God he lived and moved, and had his being: no act was done by him but in prayer: every blessing was received with thanksgiving to God,—every friend was dismissed with a parting benediction. The next feature in his character was purity and simplicity, which was in fact only the result and the expression of that habitual piety towards God which dwelt in him continually. God was continually in his thoughts and he therefore ever sought for traces of God in His image, man. . . .

. . . .

"His friend Coleridge, in his 'Aids to Reflection,' designated him as a mighty wrestler for truth.

. . . .

"There was in truth no affectation in him: his peculiarities were become habitual and natural to him and it required thought and effort to avoid them; which was continually apparent to those who saw him often, and who invariably found that all his peculiarities both of manner and expression became most strongly marked when he became most animated, at which time it is obvious that a man is most natural: he forgets to be affected in proportion as he becomes animated.

. . . .

"Coleridge had a mind which could only be fully appreciated by one of similar capacity and power, and this he found in Edward Irving; it therefore became as great a delight to the one to impart as to the other to receive. And it is not easy to ascertain whether Coleridge most loved and respected Irving or Irving, Coleridge: each has recorded his high estimation of the other,—Irving in the dedication of his missionary sermon, Coleridge in the notes to his 'Aids to Reflection.' . . .

"The lessons he taught Irving enabled him to bring at once into practical bearing upon theology and upon morals all the deepest truths of philosophy,—the matured results of a long literary life, devoting almost exclusively to metaphysical research a mind of unusual comprehension and accuracy.

"The effect became immediately apparent in a course of sermons on the Trinity, which were preached in Hatton Garden, though not published till many years after, and when Mr. Irving had removed to Regent's Square. Those discourses were delivered when his popularity was at its zenith, and received by all with the greatest applause, and produced in multitudes an effect which has abiden to the present time. None could see then anything but truth, and beauty, and orthodoxy, in those discourses which are now stigmatized as heretical and dangerous by a very large portion of the religious world.

"These animosities will now, in some measure, subside: Edward Irving is gone to his rest, and the survivors have taken their stand on one side or the other. But the truths which he proclaimed will not die with him,—they will be only the more dearly cherished by those who knew him; and they may perchance be listened to by many who knew him not, but who had imbibed from others a prejudice which made them reject everything which came from Edward Irving."

Quoted from *Fraser's Magazine*, January, 1835.

"IN his view, spiritual discernment was a nobler faculty than intellectual perception, and devotional fervor took rank before theological acumen. . . .

. . . .

"Irving very distinctly set forth that religion had broader foundations than intellectual power to rest upon; that the spiritual discernment was a faculty as active in the soul as intellectual perception in the mind; and that childhood had its power of being religious as well as manhood. . . .

. . . .

"Edward Irving is one of the most difficult writers we are acquainted with to tear oneself away from. . . .

"Irving united connectedness without its limitations to diffuseness, without its incoherences.

"Throughout all Irving's writings there runs that perfect fairness of spirit which enabled him to detect the weak points in his communion and recognized much of the excellencies of communions from which he dissented. The unsparing severity with which he used to expose the besetting faults of his co-religionists, the frank and cordial manner in which he always spoke of the Church of England as a sister church, the courageous acknowledgment which he ever and anon made of essential truth underlying the erroneous dogmas and practices of the Roman branch, distinguish him as a man of great nobility of heart."

A Churchman in the *Christian Remembrancer*. (Reprinted in *Littell's Living Age*.)

"THE depth of his habitual piety—the intimacy of his acquaintance with all the varied woes, real and imaginary, which perplex and torment the human breast—the tenderness and love with which he would listen and enter into all the niceties of sorrow—the delicacy with which he would minister to the mind diseased, and afford relief and consolation—none but his flock, and the many hundreds who applied to him, especially clergymen of the Church of England from all parts of the kingdom, can really appreciate. It is small praise to say that ofttimes has he fasted, whilst the food prepared for himself was sent to his poor brethren, who were ignorant of the quarter whence their wants were supplied; but he entered into all the necessities of every individual of those over whom he presided, temporal and spiritual; so as to make them his own—wept with their sorrows and rejoiced in their joys, as the fondest parent over the most endeared offspring. He was never heard to speak an unkind word of any of his numerous opponents, far less of any of his friends; he found something to commend in every child of Adam, and on this he loved to expatiate. He opened his heart, and with it his house and hand, to every one who came in his way; and although he hugged many a viper to his bosom, the baseness of one did not make him shut up his compassion against the rest of his kind. At no time or place or company, or circumstance, was he otherwise than as a minister of God; he entered into the full importance of the idea of being an ambassador from heaven, and he was never asleep on his post. His conversation and presence threw a sanctity over every society into which he entered; and none could cease for an instant to be conscious that there was a servant of God in the midst of them. . . .

"His defense before the Consistory of London was a masterpiece of eloquence and reasoning; and there was not a lawyer present who was not convinced that the cause should have been determined on his side; but his judges were not selected from amongst lawyers, but from amongst his accusers and executioners. The church which cast him out signed its own condemnation, when all her ministers attended his funeral as the obsequies of a minister of Christ. . . .

. . . . . .

"It is doubtful if the death of any other individual could have produced the deep, though not clamorous grief, in so many manly breasts as has been now experienced; each of whom will say, 'Multis flebilis occidit, nullis flebilior quam mihi.' "

From an article printed beside Carlyle's "Eulogy" in *Fraser's Magazine*, January, 1835.

"HE was not, as people once thought, puffed up with windy vanities and the poor breath of popular applause. Thomas Carlyle understands many things and many men; but he surely did not comprehend this man, his friend and brother, when he spoke of him as having swallowed this intoxication, and then 'being unable to live without it, striving to win back the tide of fashion, which had ebbed from his church, and gone to gaze on Egyptian crocodiles and Iroquois hunters.' We can see no trace of this poor craving in any part of his life. An egotist he was, but not of the paltry type. On the contrary, there was a kind of sublime humility in his egotism, like that of a Dominick or a St. Francis; and while he believed in himself, in his powers, his missions, his convictions, and scrupled not to speak of them and to deal with them as divine infallibilities, he was yet quite willing to become a nothing, if only the world would just believe with him. Hence his stout dogmatism, clothed with an appearance of reason, where that came handy and serviceable; boldly contemptuous of reason, when that would no longer avail. . . .

"Not a mere London notoriety, this friend of Coleridge and admired of Canning; not an orator Henley, or a Dr. Cumming, but verily and nobly a true servant of God. We know not what the English have thought of him, since he left them to find a resting-place in the dim, old crypt of St. Mungo's. But we can vouch for it, that in Scotland his memory has been tenderly cherished; that we are not without misgivings as to the justice of our treatment of him; and that there are far more tears dropt over his grave, than there are bitter words of his life."

Quoted from *North British Review,* Vol. XXXIX. (Attributed to Dr. Hanna, son-in-law of Dr. Chalmers.)

"BEHIND his age in many respects,—borrowing his language, his tastes, and his very spirit from the past,—seeming always more like a reproduction of antiquity than a part of the life around him,—Irving was yet before his age. He represented almost every school of present religious thought. It is not difficult to discern in him the type of the highest sacramentarianism. His theories of the humanity and brotherhood of Christ are reflected, at least, in the principles of the Broad Church school. The lowest Evangelicalism may claim him as its pattern.

"This fullness and variety of his remarkable life complicates the difficulty of forming a correct estimate of him. Some unique men are scrutable by no age. The world cannot make up its mind about them. The more it knows of their history, the more it is puzzled. Cromwell, notwithstanding Carlyle's admirable and exhaustive apology, is yet a mystery; society cannot decide whether he was a sublime and godly patriot, or a ruthless hypocrite. Bacon wears yet the twofold character of uncompromising fidelity and unprincipled time-serving. William Penn enjoys the reputation both of a saint and of a rogue. And, while some exalt Edward Irving as the grandest and most apostolic man of his day, others denounce him as the veriest fanatic.

"There is no parallel to his popularity in the history of the modern church. The success of Whitefield is not analogous. Whitefield was a preacher for the masses. He held the vast audiences which thronged to hear him spell-bound by a power which, while full of the intensest passion, and often radiant with imagination, was at the same time richly veined with popular wit, and varied with homely illustration. He had worshipers among the ranks of fashion and intelligence; but they were such as his occasional brilliance had dazzled, or his fidelity had alarmed. But Irving, with no popular adaptation, and with a stately and old-world phraseology, which gave a ponderousness to a fancy always profound, often mystical, and never precisely brilliant, achieved a success which, if not so wide-spread, was not less wonderful, perhaps more wonderful than that of Whitefield. The ministry of Whitefield had, too, the charm of novelty. Those were new truths that came flashing from his lips. He preached to a dead world and a dead Church, the Gospel of life. He was the Herald of a Divine Love, which the tens of thousands who hung upon his utterances had never heard of, or which they had, at most, regarded as a theory of philosophy, rather than a living and universal power. This was not Irving's case. He was surrounded by preachers of unquestioned fidelity and zeal. The crowds which gathered round him were made up of those to whom the Gospel was perfectly familiar. What then was the secret of his power?

. . . .

"Neither to style nor to circumstances can we attribute his popularity. He had, it is true, a majestic person. There was fascination in his flashing eye. His deep and musical voice fell with almost magic strain upon the ear. But deeper lay the secret of his power. He stood before the people less as a minister than as a prophet. He came suddenly among the Churches like some risen Moses from the hidden grave of Nebo, or like some Elijah from the burning chariot. Though a man of the future, pointing reverently onwards, he was essentially a man of the past. He spoke with the authority of him of the camel's hair and leathern girdle. His mission was not to throw the lights of recent scholarship upon the truth, or to exhibit it under its conventional aspects. The burden of his ministry was, Thus saith the Lord! With scarcely thirty summers upon his head, he pronounced his message in the language of antiquity and with the dignity of the sage. The world saw before it a prophet of God, appealing not to its passions, or its fancy, but to its reverence and faith."

Quoted from *London Quarterly Review*, Vol. XIX.

"IN a time when truth was but feebly spoken, when Christian faith was not too strong and vital, Irving stood up and spoke to his generation, and (recognizing his fit mission) to the heads and leaders of his generation —to the sages and peers and senators who thronged round him—out of the fullness of an intense conviction. And this conviction was the conviction of that truth which, in his preface to the 'Doctrine of Sacrifice,' Mr. Maurice says he learnt from Edward Irving. . . .

. . . .

"There was always in him, curiously enough, even to the last, a more than Presbyterian doggedness of devotion to the Kirk of Scotland, combined with a higher than most High Churchmen's belief in the divine origin, character, and significance of the Church, its priesthood, and its sacraments. . . .

. . . .

"When people had a cause to gain, they tried to enlist this mighty voice on their side, thinking that its utterances could no doubt be trained to the common uses and expediencies of the world, and to take its part in defending the popular compact which even Religious Societies do not disdain to make between God and Mammon. But it would not do. They take him to their Missionary Meetings, where he hears an Evangelical orator proclaiming that 'the first requisite of the modern Missionary, is prudence, and the second, prudence, and the third prudence;' and then they hear him, from the pulpit where he is asked to plead their cause, idealizing, in those stately periods which he seemed to have learnt to frame at the feet of Milton and Hooker, the picture of no modern prudent Missionary, but of the burning Evangelist, the hero of the Cross, going forth without staff and scrip, thinking nothing of subscriptions, with no vision of edified crowds in Exeter Hall, but caring only 'to spend and to be spent' in the Master's cause.

. . . .

"Thus his life-battle ended right bravely and faithfully fought through all those toilsome years in which he had seen his sublime ideas of right and truth gradually scorned and rejected by the Church and the world. He had preached righteousness in the great congregation; and Belial and Mammon were as dominant as before! He had unrolled the dark and splendid web of the Apocalypse; and

men had laughed the revelation to scorn!
He had proclaimed his Lord's oneness with
our humanity, as the root and hope of all
humanity, and the Church of his love had
branded him as heretic and traitor! He had
seen the dawning glory of 'the latter day,'
and had heard with the inward ear the very
voice of God; and the dawn had faded, and
the voice had spoken only to silence and wound
and trouble him! It seemed all a failure;
and so he died.

"We wish we could enter more fully into the
results of his life and teaching. Could we do
so, we should see how wide these results have
been,—how his teaching regarding Sacraments
and Church Orders is reproduced in the High
Churchism of England at the present day, how
his teaching regarding the restored 'gifts'
created the possibility of that new 'Catholic
and Apostolic Church,'—how his teaching regarding the Brotherhood of Christ, along with
that of Mr. Campbell regarding the Fatherhood of God, was the germ of all the deepest
teaching of the Broad Church now; above all,
how the spectacle of his life, his words and
works, was a sign to his generation, a witness
that quickened the religious life of Britain
throughout all its borders.

"He sleeps now within the crypt of the
magnificent Cathedral of Glasgow. In the

narrow window that lights his resting place a relative has placed a figure of the Baptist, portrayed with more of Christian feeling and reality of life than are common in Protestant religious art. It is a fitting mark for the grave of one who spoke and lived 'in the spirit of Elias.' Had he been laid there a thousand years ago, his tomb would have become a famous shrine."

Quoted from *Macmillan's Magazine*, Vol. VI. (Probably written by Rev. Robert Story.)

www.ingramcontent.com/pod-product-compliance
Lightning Source LLC
Chambersburg PA
CBHW062226080426
42734CB00010B/2050